START EARLY: SEX-POSITIVE CONVERSATION FOR PARENTS

HOW TO TALK TO YOUR CHILD ABOUT SEX, SEXUALITY, GENDER, CONSENT, RELATIONSHIPS, AND SAFE AND UNSAFE TOUCH TO KEEP THEM EDUCATED AND PROTECTED

ETHAN REYNOLDS

CONTENTS

Introduction   9

Part I
THE AGE-BY-AGE GUIDE

1. LAYING THE FOUNDATION   17
   Your Child and Their Growing Bodies   18
   *The Importance of Early and Open Sex
   Education*   21
   Your Role as a Parent   27
   The Benefits of a Sex-Positive Approach   31
   Setting Age-Appropriate Expectations   35
   Impact of Media and Pop Culture   41

2. NAVIGATING THE AWKWARDNESS   45
   Creating a Judgment-Free Zone   46
   Dealing With Personal Discomfort   50
   Improving Communication Style   54
   Normalizing Conversations About Sex   57
   Discussing Healthy Relationships   60

3. AGE-APPROPRIATE DISCUSSIONS   65
   *Talking to Preschoolers About Body Parts and
   Boundaries*   67
   *Navigating Curiosity and Exploration During
   Early Childhood*   70
   *Late Elementary and Pre-Adolescent Years
   (Ages 9–12)*   73
   Preparing for the Onset of Puberty   75
   *Explaining the Physical Changes in Boys and
   Girls*   78
   *Discussing Menstruation and Menstrual
   Hygiene*   82

Addressing Body Odor and Acne 84
Answering Questions About Reproduction and
Birth 86
Discussing Gender Stereotypes and Equality 90
Encouraging Healthy Body Image and Self-
Esteem 92

Part II
TEACHING SAFETY IN ALL

4. RELATIONSHIPS AND EMOTIONS 101
Different Relationship Types 103
Discussing Healthy Friendships and
Boundaries 106
Addressing Romantic Feelings and Crushes 111
Navigating Peer Pressure 114
Build Love, Trust, and Communication With
Your Kid 117
Understanding Emotions and Emotional Well-
Being 121
Discussing Healthy Coping Mechanisms and
Stress Management 125
Encouraging Open Communication Within
the Family 129

5. MEDIA LITERACY AND ONLINE
SAFETY 133
Teaching Critical Media Literacy Skills 135
Teach the Portrayal of Sex and Relationships
in Media 137
Addressing the Influence of Pornography and
its Unrealistic Expectations 141
Navigating Social Media and Healthy Digital
Habits 151
Encouraging Responsible Technology Use and
Digital Citizenship 155
Promoting a Positive Online Presence and
Respectful Behavior 157

6. CONSENT, BOUNDARIES, AND
   HEALTHY RELATIONSHIPS   163
   Defining Consent at Different Ages   165
   Discussing Consent in Different Contexts   168
   *Addressing the Role of Power Dynamics in
   Relationships*   171
   *Navigating Difficult Conversations About
   Boundaries and Consent*   175
   *Promoting Communication and Negotiation
   Skills in Relationships*   177
   *Recognizing Signs of Unhealthy Relationships
   and Abuse*   185
   *Promoting Respect and Equality in All
   Relationships*   191
   Bystander Intervention   194

7. SEXUAL HEALTH AND
   REPRODUCTION   201
   Basics of Sexual Health and Hygiene   202
   *Discussing Sexually Transmitted Infections
   and Prevention*   206
   *Explaining Contraception Methods and Their
   Effectiveness*   208
   *Addressing Questions About Pregnancy and
   Childbirth*   212
   *Promoting the Importance of Regular Check-
   ups and Healthcare*   216
   *Providing Accurate Information About
   Abortion and Adoption*   219

8. FACING CHALLENGES AND
   HANDLING TOUGH QUESTIONS   225
   *Preparing for Challenging and Uncomfortable
   Conversations*   227
   *Handling Questions About Pornography and
   Explicit Content*   231
   *Addressing Common Misconceptions and
   Myths*   233

Discussing the Potential Risks of Early Sexual Activity   236

Handling Questions About Sexual Orientation and Gender Identity   239

Providing Resources for Further Support and Information   243

Conclusion   249

References   255

YOUR FREE GIFT

As a way of saying thanks for your purchase, I'm offering the book My Body, My Rules for FREE to my readers.

To get instant access just go to:

https://upgradebookspublishing.com/Free-Gift-Ethan-Reynolds

Inside the book, you will discover:

- Promoting Body Positive
- Staying Safe Digitally
- The Power of Body Autonomy

If you want to empower your kids make sure to grab the free book.

INTRODUCTION

It can be overwhelming to raise kids nowadays, particularly when new developments in parenting and technology continue to occur daily. The task only grows harder as kids develop and must learn about often difficult subjects like sex, self-identity, boundaries, bonds, and appropriate physical contact. It's understandable to feel concerned when they are not yet ready to cope with complex scenarios. But don't worry because you possess the capacity to help them learn what they should know before venturing out further! After all, shaping their perspectives, equipping them with information, and establishing firm ground rules are essential steps toward growth.

Discussing anything related to sexuality with impressionable minds seems overwhelming. Parents might struggle with finding age-appropriate language, keeping things relatable yet scientific enough without scaring their little ones away from learning. With genuine aspirations to be the best possible caregivers by embracing child sexual development and fostering positive attitudes toward sex education, it makes sense to seek out resources geared at inspiring and equipping adult guardians. By navigating these waters together through open discussions and accessible information, everyone benefits from the enriched experience. So don't be afraid—let's take steps forward for mutual learning and closeness, starting here!

Navigating meaningful chats about such personal topics requires reliable direction and reassurance. This book simplifies concerns by breaking down conversational techniques for tackling tricky subjects while respecting unique dynamics within households. Let this book aid your endeavors by providing steady support and concrete tips for fruitful exchanges around intimacy throughout each chapter ahead! Open yourself to positive progress by turning page after empowering page. What better gift to your family than promoting heartfelt talks and well-being? Together, let's boldly explore new paths toward welcoming sex talks and stronger connections within our families!

You're not alone in finding it tough to tackle complex matters with your young ones. Many families grapple with similar difficulties, myself included. There were moments when things didn't flow smoothly for me either; yet, over time, the obstacles I faced became opportunities for growth, leading to insights and advice that could aid other parents. So please allow me to offer some guidance as one parent to another based on my personal trial and error plus professional experience. I am hoping it will help lighten any stresses related to discussing sensitive issues with your little ones.

For quite some time, I have devoted myself wholeheartedly to advancing as an expert in areas such as sex education within child-rearing. This fervent dedication has taken me on an arduous but enlightening voyage spanning half a decade, exploring new horizons in theory and reality. Through countless hours of diligent scholarship, experimentation, and actual application, my expertise has blossomed. Today, I remain fully invested in supporting your endeavors toward problem-solving amidst formative encounters surrounding intimacy and reproduction.

I wrote this book to provide you with a calming presence amid turbulence and an informed source of direction when uncertainty looms. My empathetic heart resonates with your innermost worries, born from trepidation, self-doubt, or external influences— elements that render significant conversations seemingly impossible. I stand firm, adamantly believing that by combining my tested tips with your unique strengths, we can foster successful outcomes despite such tribulations. You are not alone. Our collective journey commences today.

When talking about sex early on, kids gain clearer views about who they're becoming in the world. With a constant listening ear and permissiveness, you lay strong roots for them to interact and think through life choices as they mature. Your child grows bravely ready to deal with intricate topics like love and similar adult ideas if taught carefully earlier on in their lives. They learn that they're capable enough, too! It makes a positive difference for them long-term, equipping them to thrive even after leaving home. This caring method shapes how they treat others and act in society eventually, so let's do this to set proper examples from today forward!

In this book, you'll receive helpful pointers and insights to start these conversations calmly without upsetting little ones' feelings. Embrace a broad perspective because all sorts of folks exist under one big sky. Kids should feel seen and appreciated regardless of who they might choose to be later on down life's road. You'll read and see sample approaches that fit your youngster's personality better since every kid is special and unique. The goal? Help families to talk easily with peace and unity. Be prepared to take steps ahead toward deeper connections at home!

There is no time like the present to chat about grownup topics with kids. Teach them while they're still curious and want answers; explain tricky concepts before any outside factors confuse their pure minds too much. Start now by showing concern and support toward shaping their beliefs about bodies, affections, plus other heavy matters. Talking honestly sets the right example for future situations, leading to wiser picks when they're ready to face the big wide world. Time flies fast, but parental guidance never goes amiss—remember this crucial advice anytime doubt appears. Open hearts lead to stronger bonds with loved ones in the end.

It's time to roll up your sleeves and get your hands dirty in this important task: guiding kids through confusing issues safely and kindly. Don't be fearful or avoid the issue. Grab this book to help you figure things out along the way. Learn ways to handle different topics collectively instead of struggling alone. Raising smart individuals makes a harmonious community when they graduate into roles beyond mommy and daddy's protective care. Join forces to raise new voices eager for change; work together toward a fairer future filled with empathetic humans looking out for each other. It all starts at home, parents. Trust me, we can do this thing! Let's get started!

PART I

THE AGE-BY-AGE GUIDE

1

LAYING THE FOUNDATION

As loving caregivers, we hold immense power to cultivate our young ones' perceptions of their own body transformations. The pages ahead serve as a trustworthy companion during this pivotal period in their lives. I aim to arm you with valuable insights and guidance for engaging in meaningful discussions about intimate matters and guiding your loved ones into adolescence and beyond with poise and warmth. Join us in preparing yourself for forthcoming bonding experiences through insightful guidance and interactive exercises! Empower your whole family through shared knowledge and connection today!

Exploring the mysteries of identity and connection begins with formative conversations nurtured by listening, asking questions, and showing kindness. As we embark on the first pages of this guidebook, we plant seeds of growth in honesty and acceptance through lovingly tailored conversations and intentional actions, setting the foundation for future harmony within your cherished family unit.

Cultivating trust and companionship with your young one paves the way for fruitful interactions in sex-positive conversations. Personalized dialogues honor each child's distinctive path while strengthening their self-awareness, setting up opportunities to learn and develop. Empathetic communication helps them recognize their inherent worth and respect others' boundaries. Nourishing connections in their youth ensures a sturdy base of informed decisions and emotional intelligence for years to come. Building upon this bedrock, you establish a safe space for growth and understanding in every aspect of their lives.

YOUR CHILD AND THEIR GROWING BODIES

Embracing the transformations of your young one during puberty starts by acknowledging external shifts and inner growth. Understanding what happens within allows us to support them holistically and connect meaningfully. Examining physical changes affecting both genders alongside accompanying emotional modifications gives us insight into shared experiences and diverse expressions. By delving deeper together, let's lay a firm foundation for compassionate discussions and enduring bonds.

Physical Changes in Puberty

As you watch your kid blossom into an adult, it's vital to acknowledge their gradual physical metamorphosis, encompassing aspects ranging from height surges to sexual maturation and varying levels of hormones. Grasping this transformation allows you to tenderly escort your adolescent through various stages of discovery and personalization. Accompanying your child on their remarkable voyage reinforces mutual understanding and provides comforting security blankets throughout new encounters and emerging perspectives.

To assist your daughter in navigating her bodily changes gracefully, be attuned to variations such as menstrual commencement and increased body hair. Engaging in straightforward, affirming conversations bolsters her courageous spirit and unwavering love toward herself. Following suit, educate your son about his growth trajectory, which will entail more pronounced masculine features like vocal deepening, overall muscular enhancement, and facial or body hair evolution. Arming him with clarity fosters greater self-confidence and assuredness in handling natural shifts within and around himself.

Emotional Changes

Besides adjusting to visible bodily adaptations, puberty comes with a wave of invisible emotions. Mood swings, enhanced sensitivities, and amplified individual consciousness mark key elements of experiencing change. As parents, we have navigated this maze ourselves, and we're equipped to maintain a caring and nurturing atmosphere that encourages our children to articulate themselves, allowing us to offer consolation and understanding. Together, we can help alleviate distress by actively listening and showcasing warmth when needed.

With transformations come adjustments. Your child might encounter insecurities around appearance, self-esteem, and personal definition. Ensure they have a non-judgmental space where words flow freely, emotions pour forth, and you receive their confessions with open ears. Cherish your exchanges and honor genuineness by honoring every emotion expressed in their journey toward comprehension. In doing so, we aid in constructing strong pillars of identity as they acquire strengthened mental faculties of fortitude and mindfulness.

THE IMPORTANCE OF EARLY AND OPEN SEX EDUCATION

Realizing the potential benefits of imparting thorough sexual guidance at an early age enables us to endow our kids with the expertise, poise, and judiciousness required for sound choices, appropriate boundaries, and fruitful personal explorations during adolescent growth. It strengthens their bonds with parents, enhancing openness and trustworthiness, and empowers them to handle their changing intimate needs in a constructive light. We arm our young adults with essential knowledge, tools, and resolve by exploring these dividends and engaging in proactive instruction.

Advantages in the Early Years

- **Better parent-child communication:** Starting sex talks with your kids before they reach double digits helps shape deeper ties between you and them. As you share your knowledge, interactions become meaningful exchanges where queries get resolved, hearts find solace, and attachments strengthen over time. When families engage in these intimate chats, it sets a precedent for future generations while developing shared values together.

- **Body positivity:** Navigating chats on sex and bodies helps kids recognize that beauty varies and everyone undergoes unique transformations. This awareness empowers a love for one's appearance, making body positivity come naturally before society tries to influence appearances. Equipping these foundational beliefs within them will aid their confidence and how they perceive others.

- **Acceptance of change:** Familiarity with transformative processes leads children to understand the dynamic nature of life. Learning about the adjustments triggered by maturation readies them to confront such variations boldly. Guiding youths to handle fluctuations skillfully supports personal growth and poise. Awareness rooted in early sex education equips them to face the unknown aspects of life with assurance.

- **Recognize boundaries:** Children need guidance in learning proper interaction principles like boundaries, mutual agreement, and admiration for others. Through introducing the significance of sex education, kids acquire the practical wisdom necessary for forming strong but considerate connections from a tender age. Arming youths with this fundamental expertise ensures the evolution of more inclusive partnerships later in life. Developing these attributes early sets up lasting habits based on equality and reciprocal appreciation.

- **Healthy gender identity:** Understanding and valuing varied genders is critical for young minds. Introducing and celebrating human diversity through appropriate early sex education nurtures harmony among varying identities. Such exposure enables budding generations to acknowledge multiple expressions of personhood, reinforcing the intricate balance required for constructive societal cohabitation.

- **Disclose sexual abuse:** Providing an outlet for disclosing undesired experiences plays a significant role in safeguarding kids. Early sex education provides children with essential skills for recognizing and sharing distressing events while creating a compassionate setting where incidents can be brought forth safely. With comprehension and openness, caretakers can shelter their little ones, offering unencumbered dialogues.

- **Safe from sexual abuse:** Instruction on security measures and recognizing when something feels incorrect can arm children against prospective mistreatment. Informative lessons on suitable behavior and informed consent help establish a sturdy base for detecting potentially damaging circumstances. By acknowledging these warning signs, kids learn to fend off threatening encounters or people and act proactively in troubling scenarios, thus staying better protected.

Advantages in the Teenage Years

- **Helps teens to know the safe option:** Offering extensive sex education during this phase allows teenagers to grasp all birth control techniques, as well as ways to guard themselves against transmittable diseases. Acquiring a broad spectrum of information prompts enhanced decision-making about intimate matters, inspiring safer behavior without limiting enjoyment. Enabling informed choices boosts overall well-being and minimizes potential risks associated with incomplete or misguided perspectives on sex.
- **Make smart sexual decisions:** Empowering teenagers with reliable information on sexuality, interpersonal dynamics, and

expressed agreement facilitates more prudent judgments, which they can then adapt into actions matching their individual beliefs and preferences. Presenting dependable data promotes wise decision-making around sexual topics, ultimately strengthening well-rounded development grounded in facts.

- **Sex will be safer and more consensual:** Providing insight into acceptable amorous interactions, agreements, and protected intercourse assists teenagers with maintaining respectful relationships and reduces harmful conditions. Possessing conscious awareness results in more favorable, deliberate actions, thereby cutting back the probability of unwanted developments or problems caused by a lack of information.

- **Helps teach moral values to your kids:** Exposing youth to sex education enables you to instill your ethical convictions through education that covers the mental, emotional, and physical aspects of sex. Honoring household standards alongside well-rounded wisdom creates a supportive network that encourages balanced growth and development underpinned by established morality shared between you and your growing kids.

- **Reduce the stigma that comes with sexuality:** Open discussions surrounding various types of attraction, gender variations, plus differing partnerships allow everyone to feel like valued contributors. Promoting greater appreciation fosters a broader understanding of personal expressions of love or affection. Encouraging a nonjudgmental perspective provides opportunities to live freely without fear of isolation because of unique, intimate preferences.

- **Helps teens to know the risks of having alternatives to vaginal sex:** Talking at length about multiple sex acts brings attention to the linked dangers of each form, allowing youngsters to evaluate potential consequences before making an educated choice. Fostering smart judgments decreases the chances of harmful experimentation due to ignorance or pressure from peers.

The initial discussion of sex should begin much earlier than many realize. Starting these conversations, coupled with thorough explanations and clear examples, provides the means necessary for guiding the intellectual evolution of kids. This progression continues until they reach an age when they can responsibly act on this knowledge, having garnered proficiency in appropriate conduct during romantic involvement. Establishing strong fundamentals through effective instruction is crucial for future success in navigating potentially complex or confusing social dynamics.

YOUR ROLE AS A PARENT

Parenthood grants us the privilege of molding our young one's perceptions of sexuality and relationships. Our loving guidance can positively shape them into confident and content individuals. Fostering awareness, offering tenderness, and supporting free discourse pave the pathway toward helping our growing family members blossom into confident individuals who take charge of their bodies and emotions. Tune in to discover ways to positively contribute to opening doors of safety, trustworthiness, and love throughout their lives. Keep your spirits lifted; with determination and adoration, you both got this!

Establishing Trust and Open Communication

Trustworthiness and accessible interactions rank high among our duties as parents. When we offer security and inviting dialogues, our little ones are more likely to confide in us regarding sensitive matters concerning sex, love, and relationships. Through your dedication, you strengthen a secure attachment that will serve as a sturdy framework for future experiences.

Being an Educator

Within your grasp lies the chance to assume the position of wise teacher and offer understandable insights tailored to your child's stage in life. You stand ready to simplify intricate concepts surrounding human relations and sexuality. Study credible materials to fortify your confidence when fielding questions or correcting misunderstandings. Empowering your children with precise comprehension helps them form sensible choices and adopt a balanced view of themselves and their bonds with others.

Promoting Healthy Relations and Boundaries

Forming connections involves setting limits and communicating effectively, two principles you must instill as a responsible guide. Highlighting the significance of approval, esteem, and free discourse reinforces your little one's capacity to establish and protect appropriate boundaries in every facet of life. By delving into matters like consent, privacy, and psychological welfare, you arm them with the courage to pursue meaningful bonds that showcase mutual admiration and clear dialogues. Promote a constructive outlook toward closeness by teaching these vital fundamentals.

Nurturing Positive Body Image and Self-Esteem

Your words carry weight in shaping your little ones' perspectives on themselves and the world around them. Nurture a favorable and inclusive mindset toward their bodies, allowing them to grow a sound sense of pride and self-value. Engage in dialogues focusing on positive body attitudes, diversity recognition, and self-love exercises to guide them in creating a harmonious relationship with their physiques, thereby increasing their overall joy and confidence.

Modeling Healthy Attitudes and Behaviors

By acting as an example, you exert a substantial sway on how your children perceive and interact with the world relating to intimate matters. Showcase virtues like regard, compassion, and adaptability in your own conduct, offering them a practical template to pattern their thoughts after. Expressing open and honest discourse, presenting wholesome interpersonal patterns, and upholding limits create a powerful, positive imprint in their minds, guiding them toward beneficial viewpoints and approaches in life.

Addressing Safety and Consent

In addition to being a provider and nurturer, part of your job involves protecting and preparing your young one against hazards. Educate them on individual safeguards, hazard detection, and right assertion, endowing them with the self-reliance and discernment required to thrive in various circumstances. With the backing of these fundamental abilities, they acquire the capacity to adopt safe postures when faced with challenging situations, securing their physical and emotional well-being.

Your task as a parent transcends mere data dissemination; rather, it encompasses creating a warm and welcoming atmosphere, encouraging honest conversations, and embedding values that promote dignity, consent, and enduring bonding. By donning the hats of teacher, defender, and companion, you enable your kid to confront the intricacies of eroticism, sensuality, and human interaction with poise, understanding, and optimism. Remember, your guarding, backing, and unwavering dedication to forthright and amicable correspondences shall mold their perceptions, self-regard, and ultimate happiness. Cherish this crucial duty with affection, sympathy, and a resolve to sustain receptive and caring ties.

THE BENEFITS OF A SEX-POSITIVE APPROACH

Embracing sex positivity is a liberating and encompassing method for tackling issues concerning sex, sensuality, and connections. It favorably grants individuals an inspiring, broad-minded method to discuss these aspects of life. This perspective stresses equality, the absence of preconceptions, and the encouragement of healthy dispositions regarding erotic expressions. By accepting and promoting this mindful stance, you craft an environment wherein your children may evolve a secure and appreciative comprehension of their individual sensuality, deliberate wisely, and cultivate propitious bonds. The following are the benefits of sex positivity.

- An orientation that positively regards sensual diversity engenders each person to acknowledge and accept their singular appetites, preferences, and limitations without experiencing remorse or shame. Such perspectives let children feel welcome to voice their preferences and wishes regarding their sensuality without fear or guilt. By facilitating an upbeat and accommodating ambiance where exploration and authenticity are cherished, young ones may form a strong sense of autonomy, self-approbation, and potency in articulating themselves plainly.

- If we take a sex-positive approach, there will be more positive conversations between guardians and kids. The subject of sex and loving connections becomes commonplace and inviting, and kids come to understand what is happening around them better and communicate their queries and troubles easily. It leads to a robust bond between parents and their children since everyone feels more comfortable talking together. Kids get a clearer idea about how to deal with sexual issues and grow up with a more natural and less restricted view of sex.

- Being proactive in teaching youngsters will provide them with vital experience in managing their private affairs when it comes to sexual behavior. Youngsters acquire insights into family planning methods, respectful interaction with others, and clear communication. They learn the importance of safeguarding their bodies from ill effects by saying no to dubious actions and protecting themselves during erotic contact. As such, they become proficient at taking control of their lives and making smart decisions based on their knowledge.

Consequently, the next generation evolves into sexually responsible grown-ups.

- Encouraging this outlook confronts traditional views on sexual matters and differences among people. By being welcoming to varied types of attraction, ways one sees oneself, and the means one chooses to present oneself, you teach little ones to appreciate differences and cultivate kindness and sympathetic understanding toward fellow humans. With this mentality, young souls will think more expansively about humankind and form an environment where people coexist harmoniously because of their expanded worldview.

- Teaching adolescents about affirmative agreements, fruitful conversation, and building strong boundaries in love affairs plays a crucial role in helping them construct enduring bonds. Educating teenagers about the significance of consent and admiration allows them to identify whether or not relations possess wholesome elements. It also provides youth with coping strategies should disagreeable circumstances arise. In essence, growing adults gain insight into the significance of mental well-being and forming positive associations, which have long-lasting benefits. Therefore, families benefit as

individuals grasp these important concepts
early in life.

- An orientation like this stresses the relevance of
  looking after one's intimate health and ensuring
  security. Parents educate children on STDs,
  birth control techniques, and routine
  examinations. Young people become familiar
  with the value of protecting themselves and
  their companions while having intercourse.
  Henceforth, they mature into conscientious
  lovers who practice precautions and safety.
  Overall, learning such lessons at an early stage
  benefits the whole community due to a
  decrease in unsafe behaviors leading to poor
  health conditions.

- Caring for your child's sexual maturation
  requires creating a secure space where they can
  accept what feels natural to them and find inner
  power by recognizing their intuitions. They
  learn how to take charge of their physical
  experiences so they are prepared for any social
  factors that could cause distress around their
  sexual urges. Raising your family with
  sensitivity creates robust individuals able to
  weather problems arising from intimacy
  exploration. Your thoughtful guidance is a boon
  to their existence.

When you embrace this perspective as a guardian, it has multiple advantages for your little one's welfare and progress. A welcoming attitude toward diversity combined with active promotion of informed decisions produces a nurturing setting in which your son or daughter can delve into personal inclinations, form sound attachments, and settle upon mature judgments. Don't forget, this outlook applauds originality, deepens awareness, and lays the groundwork for a content and self-empowered grown-up life filled with satisfying passionate affiliations.

SETTING AGE-APPROPRIATE EXPECTATIONS

Speaking about matters like sex and relationships calls for considering your child's growth. Be aware of their current abilities to discuss such subjects. The information given should fit their understanding level so that they comprehend it effortlessly. Age-suitable conversation guides enable a helpful ambiance in which youths grasp essential concepts. Hereafter, let us analyze why age-appropriate communication standards matter during conversations about complicated topics impacting children and how parents can design suitable frameworks based on their children's evolving necessities. We want youngsters to discover and grow safely under our care.

Talking about romance and affinity concerns should include sharing ideas according to your kid's intelligence and readiness. Ensure you do not confuse them with advanced notions too early. Starting slow when explaining things allows for a strong base of knowledge they build upon as they get older. For this reason, let me explain how approaching these chats at your child's level helps them better understand and cope with sensitive issues. Providing age-appropriate wisdom contributes to safe learning experiences. Focus on age-specific goals you can use when addressing touchy topics to guide your child through successful mental and psychological growth.

Kids advance in distinct ways as they experience changes throughout their lives. Their perception of sexuality transforms accordingly. To help them understand, we should communicate details that suit their age. That way, the information shared matches their growing capacity to grasp and relate to new insights. It makes sure kids adapt without feeling overwhelmed or bored. Children deserve conversations customized to meet their changing requirements.

Preschool Age (0–5 years)

During their pre-school days, little ones start realizing their bodies and identifying if they are male or female. At this point, we need to talk to them about understanding their bodily functions, recognizing boundaries, and knowing the correct names for each part of their anatomy. Discussing consent means teaching them that they have choices when showing affection. They may choose who gets to hold them, give them kisses, or even play with them. Children should also feel secure and trust that since their bodies belong to them, nobody has the right to touch their bodies without asking first. When speaking to them about delicate subjects, always use straightforward terms they will easily follow. Being plain-spoken also helps ease fear and apprehensions.

School-Age (6–8 years)

Once children become school-aged, their fascination with where babies come from could rise. At this juncture, offering precise facts regarding conception serves as the best course of action. Since we must use vocabulary and principles they grasp easily, concentrate on the reproductive cycle and its essential processes. We must detail where babies come from sensibly while preserving privateness and regard for one another's boundaries. Take extra care to dispel any misunderstandings to avoid confusion. Creating an environment that promotes open interaction by providing comfort guarantees that the bond between parent and child remains unbroken.

School-Age (9–12 years)

As kids transition from childhood to adolescence, their comprehension of love, intimate connections, and intercourse grows intricate. This is the appropriate time to broaden their outlook on maturity, the changes happening inside of them, as well as the psychological factors associated with romantic associations. Share details related to menstruation, nocturnal ejaculation, and the appearance of secondary sexual attributes, along with why these happen during pubescence. While doing so, continue reinforcing notions such as acquiring consent prior to engaging in sexual acts, effective conversation techniques, and admiration for individual limitations. Let's keep chatting about affection, having feelings for someone, and controlling sentiments, all while stressing fairness and acknowledging one another's perspectives. This way, we set up solid foundations for long-lasting, gratifying partnerships later on.

Adolescence (13–16 years)

Adolescence brings increased interest and experimentation with sexual matters. Now is when we must offer thorough details pertaining to reproductive well-being, birth control practices, sexually transmitted illnesses (sexually transferred conditions), and the sentimental elements present in partnerships. Make sure to cover areas like consent before taking part in sexual activities, coping strategies, and obtaining factual information from dependable channels. Assist your child in building self-confidence and independence while laying down boundaries and emphasizing accountability during their evolving experience with adult relationships. Always strive to maintain a supportive ambiance that ensures a deeper appreciation of meaningful relationships in the future. By doing so, parents can aid young people throughout this critical stage, helping guide their growth toward responsible participation in adult attachments.

General tips for all age groups:

- Use simple and familiar language that they can easily understand. Also, make sure to present concepts in ways that are appropriate for their ages and stages of development.
- Provide accurate and truthful responses to all questions, making efforts to clear up any incorrect notions that your kids may have formed.
- Establish an environment where queries can be raised comfortably without fear of reprisals, negative consequences, or ridicule. Foster a sense of openness so that discussions around

sexual health and reproduction become easy and natural.

- Pay attention closely while listening to ensure you fully comprehend their concerns and feelings. Acknowledge these sentiments and validate their perspectives. This assures that they feel understood and heard.
- Take into account each child's level of understanding, emotional maturity, as well as personal preferences before beginning or engaging in talks about sex education. Adjusting interactions accordingly helps make certain that sensitive subjects are handled at levels most suitable for every youngster.
- Always prioritize keeping confidential matters private during talks. Give kids control over how comfortable they want to feel throughout chats; allow them room to set limitations if necessary.
- For better clarification, incorporate visually appealing graphics, publications, or age-appropriate tools that complement discourse topics. These additional materials serve to reinforce a more complete understanding.

IMPACT OF MEDIA AND POP CULTURE

Due to modern innovations in technology and widespread cultural influences, media and popular traditions are incredibly influential nowadays. They significantly shape how folks perceive sexual activity, gender identification, and human bonds. Parents need to be aware that their little ones are exposed to these outside stimuli daily and learn from them as well. We'll look at how these external sources affect one's thoughts, evaluate what benefits or disadvantages arise because of this exposure, and suggest helpful approaches for assisting your child in acquiring a balanced outlook regarding love, intimacy, and sex. It is necessary for caretakers to lead by example, considering their own behavior and beliefs around these subjects.

Being familiar with how different types of media, such as TV shows, movies, songs, and social media platforms, exhibit romance and physical interactions is important. Children form opinions about these matters based on what they observe in these mediums; therefore, awareness of their presence is imperative. To help ensure productive discourse concerning what your youngster has viewed or experienced, take some time studying examples of these depictions together with them. With improved insight into how they interpret what they see and hear, you're more likely to contribute meaningfully to their education and understanding regarding sensitive issues relating to sex and interpersonal relations.

When it comes to publicizing ideas and concepts via all kinds of mass media, there can be both unfavorable and advantageous consequences that result from these kinds of depictions. For instance, there might be situations where certain groups of people might receive negative treatment or encounter false information. On the flip side, if presented correctly, media can provide suitable illustrations of assorted preferences, individual traits, and fair dealings, among others. By examining examples of these depictions jointly with your kids and sharing your thoughts about them, you can help raise their understanding of what is acceptable behavior involving people who may vary considerably from themselves.

The media frequently presents simplified versions of life that do not necessarily match reality. Many of these accounts tend to repeat inaccurate facts or exaggerate situations so they might appear appealing to viewers. The tendency to generalize or oversimplify complex concepts is prevalent across most genres of entertainment. Although they're intended to captivate audiences, it's possible to find elements that don't align with reality. Therefore, it's crucial to approach things critically and carefully analyze whether details seem reliable before accepting them. One way adults can aid children in doing this would be to clarify things when watching films or programs collectively and ask kids thoughtful questions afterward to check their understanding of what was depicted. Examples like these offer opportunities for teaching children valuable lessons that benefit them later on as responsible members of society.

If youngsters learn basic principles governing mass communication, they acquire practical knowledge useful for making sense of everyday encounters. Teaching your children to assess media presentations ensures they recognize underlying motivations for why products are marketed in specific ways. They also become adept at determining how data is organized to create persuasive impressions. This enables them to make informed decisions when selecting items to watch or listen to. Understanding these fundamentals empowers children to establish their own beliefs and attitudes, rather than merely accepting things at face value without questioning them.

Young children should observe reasonable limitations concerning the amount of time spent focusing on displays since excessive exposure could compromise their overall development. Adults who supervise these youths have a responsibility to ensure that screentime doesn't interfere too much with other essential components constituting a balanced lifestyle, such as personal contact along with pursuits that challenge mental faculties plus bolster emotional wellness. Restrictions must target maintaining an equilibrium between on-screen pastimes plus alternative actions crucial for optimal living.

Dealing with sex talk with kids can be tough, but remember, you are not alone! Understanding how the media affects us can help make things easier. The media doesn't always accurately portray what real life looks like. When talking to your child, be aware when images might be confusing or incorrect. Remember, they're still developing, and unhealthy ideas could stick with them over time. Help promote a kinder and more accurate portrayal of all people by highlighting diverse stories. Take note: These helpful resources are meant to support your amazing work already happening. Talking helps clear misconceptions and provides a comforting bond of shared knowledge.

2

NAVIGATING THE AWKWARDNESS

Navigating the subject of sex education with your young ones may initially trigger feelings of anxiety and nervousness. Trust me, you aren't alone in facing these doubts and fears. In fact, many parents hesitate when approaching this significant aspect of their little one's life journey. Nonetheless, it's necessary to acknowledge that having honest conversations concerning sexuality and relationships helps mold your youngster into a responsible and content individual. Breathe deeply and take solace in knowing that with this book, the path toward a more confident and loving bond with your family begins earlier.

Are you ready to overcome the awkwardness associated with talking to your child about sensitive topics? This chapter has got you covered! Get set for practical methods and handy pointers to demystify those tough conversations and cultivate strong and secure connections with your loved ones. Embrace this opportunity to build a foundation for honest and nurturing interactions that leave a lasting impact. Keep reading, dear parent, keep reading!

As we venture deeper into understanding effective communication around sex education, it's essential to understand that feeling self-conscious or uncertain is completely ordinary. Admitting these feelings empowers you to work through them, opening doors to smoother interaction with your kiddo. But why do these emotions surface in the first place? Societal hindrances coupled with private reservations often contribute to making us squirm when talking about physical matters. Nevertheless, identifying the root causes enables you to tackle them head-on and facilitate a harmonious exchange.

CREATING A JUDGMENT-FREE ZONE

Creating a judgment-free zone is vital when broaching delicate matters of sexuality and interpersonal connections with our children. Not only are we responsible for sharing insight and guidance, but we also have to promote an atmosphere in which our youngsters feel comfortable, included, and secure when discussing these sometimes tricky issues. In this section, you will discover why nurturing an accepting environment is necessary and receive valuable tips to facilitate productive conversations with your kids, minus any negative associations or biases. By following these suggestions, you can build strong family ties while ensuring both emotional safety and healthy understanding.

Embracing Acceptance

To construct a judgmentless setting, one needs to start with grasping acceptance. Realize that every child goes through exclusive circumstances, has particular queries, and possesses distinct standpoints. Be willing to pay attention and interpret them without being influenced by prejudiced opinions. Demonstrate understanding results in surroundings where young people can voice themselves freely and confidently.

Setting Aside Personal Beliefs

Guiding our children according to our beliefs is natural for parents, but it is also imperative to distinguish between our individual perspectives and the discourse we maintain with them. Permitting our children to contemplate and shape their own views gives them room to expand their consciousness independently. Encouraging this independent reflection allows them to grow into well-rounded individuals who possess mature viewpoints, thanks to your unbiased influence. By placing our private principles aside during family deliberations, we enable a more wholesome and open ambiance where honest interactions blossom.

Practice Active Listening

Actively tuning in to what our children think and sense is an incredibly effective technique for making a no-prejudice environment. During exchanges centered around sex and close relationships, allocate total concentration, make eye contact, and utilize gestures to confirm that you're completely engaged. This reveals to your loved ones that their ideas warrant consideration and they matter. Such active interest empowers a more peaceful home life and increases communication skills and mutual regard.

Avoid Criticism and Shame

Banishing criticism and shame creates a safer and kinder habitat. Refraining from using critical statements prevents causing hurt and promotes open conversation instead. Applaud honesty and straightforwardness by guaranteeing no rebukes for curious queries. Replace critical words with warmth and acceptance, allowing everyone to be at ease within this liberated setting. You can foster a harmonious and communicative home simply by avoiding derogatory expressions!

Use Non-Judgmental Language

The phrasing you employ significantly influences how productive your talks about sexuality and connections are. In selecting your words, keep away from negative terms that cast doubt upon diverse lifestyles or groups. Use impartial, tolerant vocabulary that doesn't single anyone out. Convey genuineness and stability, and watch as your conversational climate improves dramatically! Your manner of addressing issues establishes an example of courtesy and thoughtfulness. Implement these new practices, and witness how much better everything flows! These changes might seem subtle at first glance, yet over time, you'll see exactly how substantial an impact your considerate speech patterns have had.

Provide Non-Biased and Age-Appropriate Information

Making sure your kid has non-biased information is vital for encouraging honest and beneficial conversations regarding intimate matters. Keep in mind your kid's maturity level while talking. Base discussions on factual details and research. Assure your child gets a well-rounded viewpoint so that they don't get misguided beliefs. If our kids receive reliable information, they will possess stronger decision-making skills and enhanced self-confidence when handling topics associated with physical closeness. Provide dependable knowledge right from the start, and you can expect great outcomes for both their emotional growth and overall healthiness.

Encourage Questions and Curiosity

Nourish their spirit of inquiry; motivate your child to seek answers to whichever questions they may have. Emphasize that there are no questions too sensitive to bring up and that their eagerness to learn is a good thing! Whenever children observe us praising their thirst for wisdom, they begin to perceive education as something exhilarating. As a result, they are more inclined to take part in productive discussions without feeling scared to voice their thoughts.

DEALING WITH PERSONAL DISCOMFORT

It's completely normal to feel uneasy talking about delicate subjects such as intercourse, eroticism, and connections with our children. We could even feel anxious and uncertain if we are capable enough to manage those dialogues effectively. Despite our apprehensions and discomforts, it's crucial to acknowledge that we should confront and overcome these obstacles since communication plays a critical role during the intellectual growth process. Let's go through some useful methods to face our unease and become skilled communicators.

Normalize Your Discomfort

Firstly, let me emphasize that experiencing discomfort is completely normal whenever sex-related issues arise among families. Frequently, our tension originates from social prejudices, private uncertainties, or prior encounters. Acknowledging these sensations could enable us to tackle and conquer them head-on.

Reflect on Your Beliefs and Values

Self-examination helps immensely with minimizing discomfort brought upon by personal biases or ingrained perspectives connected to sexual behavior and connections. Analyzing your background, cultural influences, and individual experiences may assist you in comprehending why specific opinions cause distress within yourself. Exploring your views permits you to acknowledge and eventually deal with these underlying concerns, making you better equipped to engage with your child sincerely and conscientiously. Make the most of introspection to enhance your parental proficiency.

Educate Yourself

Be sure to arm yourself with knowledge before getting into sensitive talks with your youngster. Gather relevant data regarding topics such as intimacy, consent, love affairs, correct ways of conduct, and respectful bodily contact so you would be ready for whatever concerns come up. Look into trustworthy online sources and reading materials, or attain guidance from experienced individuals who can offer valuable insights applicable to different phases of development. Being familiarized with all these subjects could raise your confidence levels while talking with your kid, hence leading to a fruitful conversation. Ensure that your awareness stays up-to-date!

Start Small and Take Gradual Steps

Overpowering anxiety can sometimes discourage us from starting an interaction with our children pertaining to sex-associated matters. Beginning with fundamental ideas is always advisable; for example, you could describe certain human physiology features, discuss healthy restrictions, or explain diverse sentiments kids could encounter at particular ages. Gradually introducing additional intricate concepts linked to sex, romantic relationships, or psychological and physical boundaries enables you to monitor progress as well as adapt according to your child's readiness level. Keep in mind that talking about such areas is never finished, and proceeding at one's own pace ensures productivity. Don't hesitate to initiate these types of conversations bit by bit whenever you find them suitable.

Practice Self-Compassion

It's essential to treat oneself gently while grappling with complicated dialogues about affection and physical interactions between adults and minors. Recognize that inner turmoil actually signals your commitment to developing new expertise and competencies. Grant yourself permission to err every now and then, seek assistance, and keep studying together with your child. Appraise your attempts, even if it entails simply having started. Allow room for modesty, recognize your achievements, and congratulate each other following the advancement.

Focus on Your Child's Well-Being

Rearrange your concentration from your private distress to your kid's welfare. Realize that exploring these matters is critical for their holistic improvement and understanding. Being prepared to tackle challenging subject matters symbolizes your strong desire for their enriched upbringing and security. Adopting this outlook will allow you to conquer any internal struggles, ultimately setting the stage for forthright and caring exchanges between guardians and their children. Foster an atmosphere where both of you can thrive!

IMPROVING COMMUNICATION STYLE

Excellent rapport construction depends greatly on proficient intercommunication. Whenever broaching contentious issues like love or intimate connections, the way parents articulate themselves significantly impacts how their children understand and respond to them. Each parent possesses individual methods of correspondence influenced by their distinct personality traits, heritage, and past encounters.

Recognize Your Communication Style

Before embarking on fostering stronger connections between guardians and kids, especially as we venture into potentially delicate subjects such as romantic associations and intimacy, let's observe our innate ways of expressing ourselves. Everyone has their preferred manner—some might be quite assertive, straightforward, and unequivocal, whereas others may prefer less confrontational, subtler expressions, perhaps favoring understatement instead. Familiarizing yourself with your predominant mode of communication serves as an integral first step. Being aware of these inclinations helps you single out potential areas requiring betterment so you are able to adapt accordingly. While there is no correct or incorrect technique, grasping your natural proclivities enables you to adapt your method when obligatory.

Empathy and Understanding

Develop compassion and insight in your discourse with your kids. Envision things from their point of view and try to apprehend what they're feeling. Let them know that their emotional reactions are normal and accept that it's okay if you fail to relate completely. With patience and care, cultivating empathetic conversation establishes affinity and instills an ambiance of reciprocal confidence, which leads your youth to divulge their beliefs and predicaments freely.

Tailor Your Approach

Bear in mind each little one is exceptional and may react differently to certain speaking styles. Modify your strategy according to your child's singular nature, age, requirements, and so on. Certain minors may benefit from clear-cut discourses chockfull of facts, while other kids could demand a mellower fashion of verbal exchange. Adaptability in interacting aids us in bonding with our children at a higher level and crafting optimistic, fruitful interactions. Have all these aspects in mind the next time you speak with your kiddos! It makes all the difference!

Non-Verbal Communication

Non-linguistic signals have just as much significance when connecting with family members. Reflect on your postures, countenances, and vocal pitch throughout your conversations with your child. Realize that these nonverbal signals transmit information regardless of whether you mean them to or not. Displaying composure plus maintaining tranquility sends an implicit message of comfort, which promotes open discussions. Monitor these unintended physical reactions to avoid signifying indifference or distress unconsciously; it might hamper the quality of your communication.

Encourage Openness and Respect

Establish an environment of welcomingness where young people feel safe talking about their perspectives. Encourage queries, discussions, and worries to promote an atmosphere that values openness. Once they put forth inquiries, take note that you answer tactfully, exhibiting tolerance and providing suitable answers suited to their ages. Involving them in this type of interaction will enable you both to work collaboratively toward a deeper comprehension. Always handle their views reverently and never negate their ideas since it would reduce their enthusiasm for future interactions.

Practice Effective Feedback

Being receptive and giving helpful feedback is crucial during intense talks. Consider how to present comments that target behaviors rather than attacking personal traits. Ensure your remarks help build knowledge and growth by employing edifying words. Reframe critical responses using positive vocabulary that motivates better exchanges between loved ones. Keep in mind your goal should always center around creating productive discussions founded upon ongoing education and shared values between you and your kid. You will find this results in healthier relationships and closer bonds.

NORMALIZING CONVERSATIONS ABOUT SEX

Sexuality is embedded within every human existence, although the subject itself tends to trigger anxiety or embarrassment. We must overcome such feelings because sexuality is an ordinary facet of everyone's life. This is where I want to encourage individuals like you to embrace those emotions and recognize the need to address sex without being alarmed. Let's go into further detail regarding the significance of making casual conversation about this matter the norm—after all, it is integral to human experiences. Parents, in particular, have a duty to set up an appropriate setting where sex is viewed favorably and openly discussed.

Understanding the Importance of Normalizing

Normalizing conversations about sex is vital for the holistic progress of children. By establishing a hospitable environment free from judgment, you can assist your child in understanding their bodily functions, intimate connections, as well as overall sexual health. Such conversations can debunk common misconceptions concerning sex, alleviate tension, and reinforce self-confidence in managing physical intimacy and romantic associations independently. Remember, having open discussions about sex leads to a more gratifying adolescence and adult lifestyle.

Start Early and Age-Appropriate

Conversations about sex should start at a tender age. Be mindful not to overwhelm or confuse your little ones— just provide age-specific explanations according to their capacity to understand. It's crucial to initiate open dialogues before anything else so they view sex chats positively later in life. By doing this now, it sets the standard for future communications.

Use Everyday Opportunities

Create opportunities to talk about sexuality whenever possible. For example, when watching television programs, reading literature, or going through daily occurrences, try linking them to matters linked to sex. These instances may serve as good prompts for engaging in discussions. If done correctly, youngsters will come to appreciate the fact that discussing matters associated with sex is something worth embracing.

Be a Role Model

The way you approach discussions on sex can significantly influence kids. They take cues from adults, including yourself, so it's important to lead by example. Speak comfortably and confidentially while maintaining age suitability. Show that such discourse belongs squarely inside acceptable topics. Make sure your actions match your words to ensure kids perceive these kinds of interactions as beneficial and worthwhile.

Continued Dialogue

Normalizing the conversation around sex takes time and effort. Don't expect it to end as soon as your initial chat concludes; rather, consider this an ongoing journey throughout your kid's formative years. Continuous assessments and updates are essential to ensuring constructive outcomes. Keep talking and listening to each other. Give assurance that no question goes unanswered and concerns will always get addressed. Join forces to maintain open channels and work toward building trust together!

DISCUSSING HEALTHY RELATIONSHIPS

Fostering strong and healthy connections is vital for both personal growth and happiness. As nurturers, guiding our children in building solid relationships is part of our role. By engaging in open and supportive conversations about relationships, we enable our kids to form healthier connections and gain confidence in making judicious decisions. Delve into the significance of having open discussions regarding healthy relationships with your children and acquire effective communication tactics that lead to productive interactions.

Establishing a Foundation

Foster a foundation built upon reliability and straightforwardness along with your child. Construct an environment where they feel secure talking about sensitive issues connected to relationships. Let them know that you are there to listen, offer to back, and direct them as they traverse the path of apprehending strong bonds.

Define Healthy Relationships

Introduce the core features of a healthy relationship with your child. Stress upon aspects that shape healthy relationships like deference, reliability, honest communication, being considerate of others, and sharing fundamental principles. Encourage them to apply these concepts to assess the state of existing relationships among friends and future prospective loves. Instill confidence that scrutinizing their connections now prepares them for productive connections later on in life.

Identifying Red Flags

Educate your kid on how to detect red flags associated with unhealthy relations. Draw attention to actions that could point to toxic or abusive relationships, like dominance, deceitfulness, or even harsh treatment. Teach them when to raise alarms so they sense danger when interacting with peers or companions in romance. Give them assurance that they possess the right intuition to ask for assistance whenever necessary.

Communication Skills

Teach them the significance of respectful and effective communication in a good relationship. Guide them to understand key components such as giving full attention, articulating feelings, and finding peaceful solutions during times of disagreement. Urge them to voice their needs and boundaries respectfully while considering the other party's point of view. This skill set equips children with the ability to form successful interactions throughout their lifetime.

Consent and Boundaries

Foster open dialogues with kids about consent and boundaries. Emphasize the significance of esteeming individual liberties. Make clear that consent must be voluntary and wholehearted. Motivate your children to define and voice their boundaries while acknowledging the constraints of their companions. Cultivating an appreciation for dignity and self-governance will enable our children to flourish into ethical adults who acknowledge the value of autonomous choice.

Gender Equality and Respect

As you engage in meaningful conversations about gender equality and respect in relationships, challenge common expectations by advocating for fairness across genders. Encourage balanced dynamics in partnerships so children grow to appreciate varied perspectives. Support them in recognizing how valuing every individual leads to thriving communities where everyone feels heard and appreciated equally, unrestricted by traditional beliefs surrounding gender expressions.

Role-Playing and Scenarios

Engaging children in interactive activities, like role-playing and addressing hypothetical circumstances, helps them build valuable life skills. These exercises allow them to exercise decision-making, communication tactics, boundary setting, and self-confidence building. In turn, they're able to apply these abilities when dealing with actual relationship complications. As a parent, actively engage children to reflect on how they would respond in different instances and mentor them during these simulated events. Role-playing offers a fun and protected environment where they can exercise judiciousness in their thinking processes and action planning.

3

AGE-APPROPRIATE DISCUSSIONS

E mbarking age-appropriate conversations involving sex, sexuality, and relationships with kids can feel like a gentle tightrope walk for parents. Our utmost priority involves offering dependable insights tailored to their cognitive maturity. In this chapter, we will elaborate on the significance of age-appropriate discussions and accompany you through the process of gauging the depth of these integral interactions, making certain everyone leaves feeling confident and content.

It's important to keep in mind that every child grows differently, necessitating a customized approach when introducing diverse matters. Appraising their intellectual, emotive, and societal evolution helps pinpoint where their abilities lie and which level is most fitting for their comprehension. Age-appropriate conversations enable your child to remain comfortable and absorb the information, paving the road for more intricate and gratifying future discourses.

When it comes to discussing matters concerning human reproduction and interpersonal relations, it's crucial to adjust the content of those conversations according to your kid's age and level of advancement. Once they reach prepubescence, start with foundational ideas like body parts, boundaries, and consent. As they become teens, you should incorporate broader themes, including puberty, reproduction, and healthy relationships. Personalizing the information to their age allows you to impart vital knowledge that serves as a solid foundation for comprehending and appreciating life's intricate interrelationships.

Nurture your child's character by addressing moral and philosophical aspects within their intellectual range. Weave themes like autonomy, empathy, honesty, and healthy boundaries into your age-appropriation conversations to create a robust inner compass for future decision-making and profound bonding.

TALKING TO PRESCHOOLERS ABOUT BODY PARTS AND BOUNDARIES

As loving parents, nurturing our young children's understanding of their bodies and limits plays a crucial role in developing strong self-esteem and confidence. Embarking on warm and educational conversations regarding body elements is vital in guiding them to set protective parameters for their bodies with poise and pride. In this insightful discussion, let us discover efficient methods for engaging our preschoolers in body parts and limiting conversations, arming them with indispensable wisdom for owning their bodies and interactions mindfully and respectfully.

Using Age-Appropriate Language

When communicating about body parts with preschoolers, using age-appropriate language tailored to their age group is imperative for seamless recognition. Although some households prefer pet names for private regions, employing accurate physiological terminology like penis, vagina, and rectum may reduce ambiguity surrounding these parts of the body, leading to heightened ease and understanding. By adopting straightforward terminology, our kids acquire valuable awareness of their bodily components and feel secure exploring this subject matter.

Establishing Body Boundaries

Introducing straightforward guidelines can significantly contribute to safeguarding against any sexual abuse occurrences. A good illustration of instruction for this purpose might be, "It's okay only for mommy, daddy, and medical experts, like doctors and nurses, to look at your vulva during times we have to attend to you. Remember that if somebody else tries to inspect or feel you where you don't want to be touched, make sure to let me know as soon as possible."

Answering Questions With Clarity

Preschool years are characterized by natural curiosity, causing queries about their physical bodies. Be prepared to answer them clearly and straightforwardly yet succinctly without going into irrelevant particulars. Adapt your explanations based on their capacity to grasp things, offering just the appropriate information they require without being confused. Ensure they obtain the details they need without feeling overwhelmed or stressed.

Introducing Gender Concepts

You can start introducing elementary notions pertaining to gender identity when your preschool child shows increased awareness of gender distinctions. Stress that being male or female revolves around inner feelings rather than physical attributes alone. Make it understood that although females usually have vulvas and males normally have penises and scrotal sacs, these attributes do not define everyone's identities accurately. Utilize age-appropriate terminology to convey that even though most ladies have vulvas and most men have penises and testicles, some individuals might differ from these different combinations.

Normalizing Diversity

It's essential to appreciate the diversity of bodies and gender identities, focusing on acknowledging each individual is unique. Promote equality by emphasizing that no matter what someone looks like, everyone deserves admiration and respect. By applauding variations and inspiring openness and acceptance, cultivate prosperous and welcoming surroundings ideal for the growth of your preschooler's personal fulfillment.

Storytelling and Play

Employ interactive techniques such as storytelling and games to engage your little ones in conversations regarding bodies and boundaries. Include age-appropriate books and playthings that explore the significance of positive body image and explicit consent. Engage in role-playing scenarios to teach your preschool child to express their needs and to be aware when others show regard for their boundaries. These activities will not only facilitate understanding but also encourage a confident and assured mindset in your child.

Reinforcing Positive Messages

Consistency plays an indispensable part in fostering optimistic attitudes toward body positivity and consent. Celebrate your children's understanding of their body and their growing capability to voice their limitations. Show appreciation for their interest and eagerness to gain knowledge, thereby establishing a favorable connection between these crucial matters and a sense of achievement. Your loving approbation serves to motivate and strengthen their confidence in themselves and their boundaries, helping them develop a strong foundation for future interactions.

NAVIGATING CURIOSITY AND EXPLORATION DURING EARLY CHILDHOOD

Embark on a journey alongside young, curious souls in pursuit of understanding the wondrous universe surrounding us. Let's cultivate inherent curiosity during these impressionable years by studying essential knowledge that supports developing self-awareness in physical appearance, social connections, and fundamental sex education. This approach allows children to expand their perspectives respectfully and responsibly, promoting overall growth and well-being. Together, we will delve into the importance of guiding natural curiosity and discovery from an early age.

Validating Curiosity

Curiosity is ingrained into every child's essence. Encouraging it helps children grow personally and cognitively. Acknowledge and validate their queries and interests; let them appreciate that curiosity is normal and healthy. Reinforcing that it's okay to explore and seek knowledge about their bodies, associations, and surroundings boosts confidence in seeking more insights.

Promoting Body Autonomy and Consent

With care and tenderness, guide your child in grasping the essentials of self-control and seeking consent. Instilling a proper awareness of bodily autonomy prepares them to trust their inner voice and respect the limitations of those near them. Reassure your child that their physical form is their sole possession—nobody gets to interfere without their permission. Help them understand the concept of consent through age-appropriate examples and role-playing scenarios.

Modeling Positive Attitudes and Behaviors

As parents, we are our children's first role models. Demonstrating body positivity, wholesome interpersonal relationships, and constructive approaches to sexuality sets the foundation for flourishing futures. Display openness, courtesy, and unbiased discernment throughout your discussions and actions, paving the pathway for your kids to follow suit in their discovery and connections. Establishing clear boundaries, giving and receiving consent, and practicing effective communication teach valuable life skills necessary for ethical investigation and compassionate comprehension.

Emphasizing Emotional Intelligence

Empowering children with emotional intelligence is vital for their journey of discovery and connection. Nurture their ability to identify and communicate emotions and instill empathetic values that cultivate thoughtfulness toward others. Through emotional intelligence, your child gains essential skills necessary for building strong connections and understanding personal and social boundaries.

LATE ELEMENTARY AND PRE-ADOLESCENT YEARS (AGES 9–12)

Embrace the exciting journey of witnessing your child grow into a capable individual during the late elementary and pre-adolescent stages! Their bodies, hearts, and minds undergo remarkable transformations demanding thoughtful attention from parents. With love, care, and patience, you, as a parent, play an integral role in molding these developing minds by opening up conversations surrounding sex, sexuality, and relationships. Let's uncover the distinct qualities defining this period and arm you with effective tools for guiding and enlightening family talks about intimate matters!

Acknowledge Developmental Changes

Acknowledge your child's progression from the inside out. During this time, their body grows along with their curiosity to understand themselves more deeply alongside their surroundings. Appreciate and validate their mixed emotions through gentle affirmation. Ensure them that undergoing changes is normal since every step closer signifies healthy growth!

Internet Safety and Media Literacy

Leverage modern advancements while protecting the kids. Since accessing the web and social media becomes easier by the day, it's crucial to address digital security and understanding in interpreting mass media. Instill awareness regarding confidentiality, suitable interaction methods, and identifying potential dangers associated with unfamiliar persons lurking behind screens. Empower kids to think critically, recognize wholesome representations, and practice conscientious use of technological assets.

Addressing Bullying

Remember that this period might bring challenges like peer pressure and bullying. Prepare your growing children to tackle such scenarios head-on with smart coping methods derived from self-assurance and healthy judgment. Guide them to cultivate compassion while reinforcing their opinions. When faced with bullying, urge them to reach out securely to reliable adult mentors. By taking these steps together, we ensure that our kids acquire the strength and know-how to traverse challenging situations with confidence and kindness.

Building Self-Esteem and Body Positivity

Instruct your child to see the wonderful person within themselves, celebrating their unique traits and abilities. Nurture body positivity by shifting their concentration toward internal characteristics over external appearances. Explore together how societal stereotypes might shape perceptions of appearance, ultimately shaping more balanced views about true loveliness, which originates from one's innermost essence.

PREPARING FOR THE ONSET OF PUBERTY

Embarking on the journey of puberty can feel exciting but daunting for a precious young girl. As a parent, it's vital to offer comforting and educational surroundings. You have the power to make this transitional phase enjoyable and insightful as she discovers more about herself. Throughout this topic, we will dive into ways to approach impending pubertal transformations and promote cheerful conversations about menstruation.

Talk About Menstruation Before She Gets Her Period

As parents, we want our daughters to feel prepared and informed about important changes happening in their bodies. One key aspect of preparation involves having open and informative discussions regarding menstruation. Ideally, these conversations should start taking place several months before the actual occurrence of her first period. These chats should involve basic facts about periods, including how they work and why they happen, presented using age-appropriate language. Take time to listen and respond thoughtfully to any queries or uncertainties she may have; being responsive to her needs helps build trust and ensures positive interactions moving forward.

Give Your Daughter the Supplies She Will Need

Encouraging your daughter to embrace the readiness mindset is crucial. This includes helping her acquire the necessary tools for managing menstruation once she starts experiencing her period. Present her with an array of options, like pads, tampons, or menstrual cups, allowing her to discover which one suits her preferences best. Explaining safe usage methods for each item provides peace of mind while also teaching her how to look after her body during those special days.

Keep the Talk Lighthearted

Keep conversations surrounding menstruation with a lighthearted and positive tone, which communicates healthy attitudes and reduces worry. Framing monthly cycles as something natural and integral to femininity boosts your daughter's self-esteem and promotes optimism. With this mindset, she perceives periods as a standard aspect of growing up rather than a cause for fear or discomfort.

Help to Calm Fears

When it comes to managing menstruation, expectations often differ from reality, causing discomfort, misunderstandings, or even fear. Be sensitive to your daughter's feelings and thoughts. Clarify any confusion between myth and truth. Let her know the usual effects of hormonal fluctuations like cramping and emotional shifts so she isn't alarmed by temporary discomforts. Normalizing these occurrences encourages communication and promotes problem-solving together.

Maintain Open Communication

Open, honest dialogue fosters understanding and mutual growth for both your daughter and yourself as she navigates adolescent development. Foster empathetic communication by welcoming her perceptions, questions, and aspirations with nonjudgmental attention. Through active listening and advice dispensed prudently, she gains insight into herself while acquiring support tailored to her unique circumstances.

Seek Additional Resources

Dealing with unfamiliar aspects during adolescence preparation might demand additional information. Seek aid via dependable sources outside your purview. Books, online material, and qualified medical experts deliver suitable content adjusted to your child's level of cognition. These resources contribute depth to your conversation and broaden her awareness.

EXPLAINING THE PHYSICAL CHANGES IN BOYS AND GIRLS

Embarking upon the exciting journey of adolescence alongside your growing children is both nurturing and rewarding. During these transitional years, children's bodies undergo significant transformations. Discussing these physical changes with sensitivity, compassion, and enthusiasm paves the way for confidence-boosting experiences. We will uncover effective methods for guiding boys and girls alike through these milestones with grace and strength.

How to Explain Puberty to Your Girl Child

When discussing puberty with your daughter, it's important to address the changes specific to girls. Here are some key points to consider:

- **Note the changes that are peculiar to girls:** Explain the physical changes that occur during puberty. Breast growth, increased height, facial hair, and periods mark the advent of womanhood. Remind her of the natural progression unfolding within her own body and encourage celebration of these milestones!

- **Educate her on how to deal with those changes:** Nurture your daughter's self-care practices along with her transformation into womanhood. Guide her through maintaining cleanliness and hydration levels, incorporating gentle skin routines into her schedule. Don't forget to equip her with knowledge about maintaining menstrual hygiene and selecting products (pads or tampons) based on preferences.

- **Teach her how to deal with peer pressure:** Share the significance of standing strong on her own while resisting the urge to compare herself with peers. Help her discover the beauty in her distinct path through life and reinforce that growing into puberty takes place on a schedule exclusive to every individual.

- **Teach her how to deal with boys:** Introduce the theme of male attention and desire that comes during puberty. Work together to strengthen her voice and decision-making skills, allowing her to articulate needs and expectations effectively. Guide her to recognize and maintain barriers, ensuring healthy boundaries in relationships and courtship behaviors.

How to Explain Puberty to Your Boy Child

When discussing puberty with your son, it's essential to focus on the changes specific to boys. Consider the following points:

- **Take note of the changes that are peculiar to boys:** Ensure he fully comprehends key bodily adjustments he or his friends may undergo, including rapid height increases, vocal pitch modifications, hair sprouting, and expanded muscular build. Reinforcing that these adjustments are an ordinary element of transforming into a young adult could boost comfort levels while alleviating any confusion he might have.
- **Educate him on how to deal with those changes:** Guide him toward maintaining a clean, presentable appearance while nurturing healthy habits. Emphasize critical self-care practices, ranging from skilled skin management to general cleanliness maintenance, all bolstered by routine showers. In addition, encourage engagement in fitness regimes and balanced nutrition plans. When he

adopts wholesome practices early, not only will he acclimate smoother physically, but mentally too, developing a lasting commitment to sustaining overall wellness as he moves through his teenage years.

- **Teach him how to deal with peer pressure:** Uncover the effects of outside opinions and cultural norms when navigating crucial decision-making processes. Advocate for authenticity, guiding your son in being confident and sure of himself, even when confronted with group pressures. He should look out for reliable allies and select responsible influences to model after as he grows up and solidifies his identity.

- **Teach him how to deal with girls:** Foster recognition of girls' attractions or fascination during puberty transformation. Teach him how to implement virtuous behaviors within relational interactions, highlighting respectful actions, consented exchanges, and heartfelt discourse. Strengthen compassionate character traits by stressing consideration for fellow human beings.

DISCUSSING MENSTRUATION AND MENSTRUAL HYGIENE

Introducing menstruation and appropriate hygiene practices to your daughter is an opportunity to boost her self-awareness and agency. Framing the topic in a loving and informative manner allows her to encounter menstruation with assurance and handle cleanliness methods effectively. Throughout this section, we will explore typical adolescent queries girls may have about menstruation, along with pointers on successful inter-action regarding proper menstrual hygiene. When discussing menstruation with your daughter, be prepared to address her questions and concerns. Here are some common questions she may ask:

- **What is menstruation?** Help her grasp the significance of regular menstrual cycles and their connection to fertility. Emphasize that menstruation is a normal part of female life stages wherein the womb lining is discharged to prepare for the ability to have children in the future.
- **When will I start my period?** Make sure to tell your girl that the timing varies among individuals. Normally, the onset ranges between the ages of nine and sixteen but

remind her that every single human experiences different milestones in life. There is no need to feel pressure to fit into societal constructs or measure herself against peers; embrace the diversity of the journey to womanhood.

- **How do I prepare for getting my period?** Help her prepare adequately for managing menstruation, including having essential items close at hand. Walk her through choosing suitable absorbency options, whether pads or tampons and demonstrate correct usage. Explore the significance of hygienic management techniques during this time. Don't forget to mention carrying backup supplies when venturing out, just in case unforeseen situations arise. This proactive approach sets her up for stress-free transitions through menstruation.

- **Does it hurt to get your period?** Let her know that while mild discomfort might occur for some girls, that doesn't mean everyone undergoes it. If she feels any soreness, calmly share that over-the-counter medications, heating devices, or other coping mechanisms could bring relief. Acknowledging these possibilities without causing alarm supports her overall feeling of control and comfort during her period.

- **What happens if I start my period at school?** Clarify to her that being at school when menstruation starts isn't unusual, and staff members understand how to assist students who require amenities or attention. Tell her to confide in a trusted teacher or school nurse if she requires aid or sanitary products. It's essential to emphasize that menstruation shouldn't evoke shame or humiliation since it arises naturally within all ladies.

ADDRESSING BODY ODOR AND ACNE

Children transitioning into puberty often encounter physical adjustments like body odor and acne. Although perfectly normal, these changes may lead to emotional distress or anxiety. With appropriate advice and backing, however, parents can empower children to tackle body odor and acne effectively. We will discuss simple steps toward better cleanliness, introduce personal care products, and offer encouragement throughout this transformative stage.

Maintaining Good Hygiene

Maintaining proper hygiene habits plays a vital role in preventing body odor and acne. Stress the value of everyday cleaning to your child by advocating consistent bathing or showering. Daily rinsing can eliminate perspiration, impurities, and microbes from the skin, lowering the probability of body odor and acne breakouts. Educate your child about utilizing gentle soaps or cleansers when scrubbing their bodies. Focus on those zones inclined to perspire, like underarms, groin, and feet. Make sure they rinse correctly afterward, eradicating any residue from soap. Reinforce the importance of wearing clean clothes, specifically underwear and socks. Persuade them to change clothes frequently, primarily after physical activities. Select materials composed of pure, well-ventilated textiles, such as cotton, that permit air movement and decrease moisture accumulation.

Introducing Deodorant and Antiperspirant

To help your growing child cope with increased sweat production during puberty, consider presenting them with over-the-counter (OTC) antiperspirants or deodorants designed for teenagers. Convey to them that many individuals use OTC products to combat body odor, which is something quite typical amid the developmental journey. Ensuring your child comprehends using antiperspirants or deodorants isn't unusual. Offer assistance choosing items created for your child's particular age group and skin sort, keeping away from possibly harsh chemical substances, including synthetic ingredients or scents. Explain to your child the best ways to implement these merchandise properly, beginning by getting rid of existing perspiration using a soft cloth, then lightly massaging the merchandise onto each armpit until finally dry.

ANSWERING QUESTIONS ABOUT REPRODUCTION AND BIRTH

Children possess an innate tendency toward curiosity, driving them to wonder about various aspects of existence, like how life begins and how babies are born. When discussing reproduction and the birthing process, approaching the subject matter in an amenable and sincere way is crucial. The purpose here is to delve into how to adequately respond to frequent concerns related to reproduction and childbirth in an empathetic and enlightening manner, allowing your children to develop a balanced awareness of human reproduction within a nurturing environment. As parents and guardians, our primary objective should be to encourage knowledge through transparent discussion, facilitating future growth while comfortably navigating often sensitive topics together.

Where Do Babies Come From?

Kids have a natural desire to make sense of things around them, and some could ask, "Where does a baby come from?" These instances offer chances to provide children with relevant, mature content pertaining to human reproduction. Children's ages determine the level of detail provided regarding reproduction. You can explain that babies are created when a male sperm fuses with a female egg, which usually happens during sexual intercourse.

Can Teenagers Have Babies?

Although it is physiologically possible for teens to conceive kids, it is necessary to address the responsibilities and difficulties linked to fatherhood or motherhood as minors. Highlight the significance of emotional and financial readiness needed for raising a child, along with the advantages of delaying pregnancy or parenting until they reach full maturity. Waiting longer enables youthful parents to establish themselves better prior to accepting the immense duty of supporting another person throughout their entire lifetime.

How Can People Have Babies if They're Not Married?

Having children doesn't mandate marriage. People can opt to raise children irrespective of wedlock standing. It's essential to explain that emphasis must be placed on the affection, dedication, and constancy offered by parents to their children regardless of their marital status; thus, a loving home environment remains just as viable for both single and married parents alike.

Do All Boys Have Penises and All Girls Have Vaginas?

Nature has a way of deciding that most boys are born with penises and most girls with vaginas, but the reality is so much more textured and nuanced. It's critical that we recognize and celebrate gender diversity, as not everyone fits into these binary categories. By having conversations with children about how some individuals may not identify with the gender norms usually associated with their biological sex, we can break down barriers and foster understanding. Every person deserves acceptance and respect, regardless of their gender identity.

Do You Have to be Married to Have Sex?

Love and lust don't require a marriage certificate. But to make sure that delighting in intimacy with another person is a fully conscious and empowering experience for all involved, there are crucial topics to tackle. It's important to explore the concept of consent along with the importance of cultivating healthy relationships. Emphasizing responsible decisions about sexual behavior and the use of contraceptives can prevent unwelcome surprises like unintended pregnancy and sexually transmitted infections.

How Do Two Moms or Two Dads Have Sex?

Combat queries about same-sex couples and their physical relations with a sensitive, inclusive, and thoughtful approach. Articulate that the physical exchange of affection between two people, irrespective of their gender identity, is an intrinsic and beautiful indication of love and attachment. Zero in on the significance of cultivating love, respect, and open communication—the bedrock of every wholesome and fulfilling relationship, irrespective of its nature.

What are Condoms?

When broaching the topic of contraception, particularly condoms, convey their crucial role in preventing unintended pregnancies and shielding against sexually transmitted infections. Imperatively, distinguish condoms as a barrier method of contraception that is available to both males and females. Highlight the paramountcy of employing condoms consistently and correctly to optimize their effectiveness.

DISCUSSING GENDER STEREOTYPES AND EQUALITY

In the current era, promoting gender equality and challenging long-standing gender stereotypes has become increasingly essential. By fostering unrestricted and optimistic discourses with your child, you can facilitate their understanding of the significance of gender equality and inspire them to shatter prejudice and limiting beliefs. Let's delve into techniques to address gender stereotypes and stimulate equality in a constructive and uplifting way.

Challenging Gender Stereotypes

Empower your child to question and challenge the gender stereotypes they encounter. Enlighten them about the fact that interests, abilities, and attributes aren't defined by gender but are indicative of individual predilections and strengths. Familiarize them with a wide array of role models representing varied genders who inspire them to shun traditional gender norms. Demonstrate instances of accomplished men and women pursuing a wide range of interests and careers beyond the narrow confines of societal expectations. Train your child to show compassion and kindness to all, irrespective of subjectivity. Impart in them the sense of equality—to acknowledge that every individual deserves a fair chance and must be judged based on merit, skills, talents, and character, and certainly not on gender identity.

Promoting Gender Equality

Unleash in your child the profound significance of affording equal opportunities to all, irrespective of gender differences. Let them fathom that everyone deserves to pursue their dreams and aspirations without gender-based restrictions. Create in them the conviction to propagate sensitivity, respect, and mutual agreement in every encapsulation. Highlight the indispensability of treating individuals with absolute equality without succumbing to discriminatory practices or imposing power struggles based on gender. Encourage your child to partake in gender-oriented conversations about familial and societal obligations and responsibilities. Enlighten them about the universal truth that household chores, vocational choices, or even caregiving responsibilities lack gender limitations and must be distributed based on abilities and penchant.

Addressing Gender Questions

Nurture a safe and supportive environment for your child to open up about gender identity queries. Enlighten them on the deeply individual experience of gender identity and instill the importance of upholding and accepting each individual's self-identified gender. Empower your child with the essential attributes of inclusivity and reverence toward individual gender orientation. Reinforce in your child the intrinsic value of treating every person with dignity, kindness, and empathy, irrespective of their gender identity or expressive mannerisms. Guide your child in analyzing and challenging the gender stereotypes that run rampant in media and pop culture. Encourage them to question the limitations laid out for individuals based on gender and to celebrate and appreciate diverse gender representations.

ENCOURAGING HEALTHY BODY IMAGE AND SELF-ESTEEM

The world often reinforces impossible and idealistic standards of beauty while perpetuating a negative self-image. Hence, it is our crucial responsibility to erect support systems that facilitate healthy body image and bolster our children's self-esteem. Radiating positively toward their physique and cultivating an accepting essence will equip them to embrace their distinctiveness and encourage them to kindle their self-love.

Teaching Body Positivity

Introduce to them that the rhythm of everybody forms a symphony of uniqueness and beauty that cannot be mimicked. Teach them that the idea of a perfect body type is a myth and that every form and pigment holds its charm. Help them explore and appreciate the inner workings of their bodies by accentuating their strengths and capabilities. Discuss with your child about media and societal norms and how they can paint an illusive image of beauty that does not truly represent reality. Empower your child to discover their own essence of beauty through the lens of individuality and character.

Avoiding Body-Shaming

As a parent, be the conductor of positivity and avoid the harsh notes of negativity regarding your child's or others' bodies. Mind the words you choose and the meaning they convey about the human body and its appearance. Let's shift the focus from measuring weight and size to embracing overall wellness and a sense of serenity that emanates from within. Nourish your child's body, mind, and soul with wholesome food, physical activity, and self-care routines. Help your young champ to develop self-assurance and esteem by highlighting their strengths and distinct qualities.

Inspire them to confront pessimistic thoughts, opt for self-affirmations, and practice self-compassion.

Preventing Comparison

Empower your children by instilling in them a vibrant perspective that each person is unique in their own way and that it's unfair to compare oneself with others. Teach them to harness their individuality, relish their exceptional traits, and cherish their accomplishments. Shift the focus from mere physical characteristics to innate qualities, skills, and victories. Encourage them to acknowledge and celebrate their unique strengths, passions, and achievements. Fuel their gratitude with self-care routines that bolster their well-being, motivating them to cherish their bodies. Teach them the significance of nutritious food, ample rest, and activities that make their heart soar with delight.

Teaching Body Care

Inculcate the essence of self-care in your child, highlighting the significance of immaculate hygiene, plentiful slumber, and an active physical lifestyle. Kindly assist kids to discover and express themselves through numerous means, like their fashion sense, artistic side, or athletic pursuits. Inspire them to dress up in an attire that exudes comfort and confidence. Enlighten your child that real beauty stems not just from the outer frame but also emanates from virtues like compassion, empathy, and grit. Galvanize your child to cultivate these inner assets with zeal and passion.

CHAPTER "GOOD WILL"

Helping others without expectation of anything in return has been proven to lead to increased happiness and satisfaction in life.

I would love to give you the chance to experience that same feeling during your reading or listening experience today...

All it takes is a few moments of your time to answer one simple question:

<u>Would you make a difference in the life of someone you've never met—without spending any money or seeking recognition for your good will?</u>

If so, I have a small request for you.

If you've found value in your reading or listening experience today, I humbly ask that you take a brief moment right now to leave an honest review of this book. It won't cost you anything but 30 seconds of your time— just a few seconds to share your thoughts with others.

Your voice can go a long way in helping someone else find the same inspiration and knowledge that you have.

Are you familiar with leaving a review for an Audible, Kindle, or e-reader book? If so, it's simple:

If you're on **Audible**: just hit the three dots in the top right of your device, click rate & review, then leave a few sentences about the book along with your star rating.

If you're reading on **Kindle** or an e-reader, simply scroll to the last page of the book and swipe up—the review should prompt from there.

If you're on a **Paperback** or any other physical format of this book, you can find the book page on Amazon (or wherever you bought this) and leave your review right there.

https://amazon.com/review/create-review/?
&asin= B0CV4GMHJD

PART II

TEACHING SAFETY IN ALL

4

RELATIONSHIPS AND EMOTIONS

O ur expedition on this earth calls for honing fundamental skills such as building genuine relationships and attuning to our emotions, which are pivotal for our holistic well-being and happiness. As guardians, it lies in our hands to steer our children toward developing these crucial abilities. In this chapter, we plunge into the significance of guiding our children toward handling relationships and emotions so they can cultivate fulfilling connections and underline the significance of their emotional vigor. This chapter acts as a Wayfinder to bolster you in navigating your child's development, fostering harmony and emotional wellness in your melodic journey of life.

Nurture your child's emotional intelligence by encouraging them to express their feelings. Bolster channels of positive expression, such as creative endeavors like journaling, painting, or heartfelt chats. Lead by example and guide them in formulating techniques to best navigate emotional turmoil. Instill wholesome coping mechanisms, such as controlled breathing, mindful exercises, and seeking counsel from confidants. Assure your child that every emotion they experience is valid and normal. Build an environment of comfort and resilience where your child feels secure to freely communicate without fear of bias or rebuke.

Instilling in your child the importance of self-care habits that champion their emotional wellness is an excellent investment in their overall growth. Foster and endorse activities that give them a sense of joy, such as physical exercise, spending time with serene nature, or practicing their interests. Your child should understand that expressing their emotions candidly is perfectly fine. It is vital to teach them that being vulnerable is actually a show of inner strength, and reaching out to trustworthy people can greatly aid their emotional fortitude. Encourage your child to confidently seek help when they need it, as this demonstrates courage and resilience. They should be aware that there are professionals and dependable adults who can guide and support them.

DIFFERENT RELATIONSHIP TYPES

Relationships are like a spectrum, with each type bearing its own dynamics, expectations, and levels of commitment. To teach your kids about embarking on the journey of building relationships, it's essential to acknowledge and teach the various forms of relationships. From the blissful days of dating to the days of committed relationships, the joyride of casual partnerships, the thrill of casual sex, the uncertainties of situation-ships, and the thrill of ethical non-monogamy. By embracing a positive and unbiased attitude, we can assist the kids in navigating the complexities of different relationship dynamics.

Dating

Teach them about the delightful memories dating evokes—a time of exploration and adventure, where two individuals traverse uncharted terrains discovering each other and the magic that sparks between them. This special phase is all about forging meaningful connections, uncovering shared interests and values, and testing romantic compatibility. Dating is the cosmic playfield where one can explore the promise of potential relationships while remaining open-minded and embracing opportunities for personal evolution and self-discovery.

Committed Relationship

The boundless connection of a committed relationship delves into the depths of complete emotional and amorous devotion. Such a bond often involves the essence of exclusivity, trust, and sheer determination to build a long-lasting companionship. While in a committed relationship, partners collaborate in fostering each other's personal growth and traversing hurdles while laying the foundation of a harmonious future based on true love and equitable admiration.

Casual Relationship

In an easy-breezy bond, a casual relationship relinquishes the need for long-term commitment and embraces more laid-back and flexible terms. It entails enjoying each other's presence and indulging in shared hobbies without the expectation of exclusivity or long-term commitments. To establish boundaries and steer clear of confusion, transparent and open communication between both parties is necessary for a casual relationship to thrive.

Casual Sex

Casual sex represents the glorious collaboration between two individuals who do not share a committed or romantic bond yet are mutually consensual to engage in sexual activity. It throws light on the significance of vocalizing each other's needs, granting the necessary consent, and shelling out mutual compassion. Allowing oneself to indulge in such moments of passion should always be an introspective personal choice that weighs in personal values, set criteria, and individual protection policies.

Situationship

A situationship is a peculiar sort of connection that encompasses certain romantic aspects but with an absence of well-defined labels or commitments. Each situationship may take on different undertones, with the degree of emotional attachment and commitment varying from one person to the next. The key to managing these uncharted territories of the heart lies in open channel communication, valor in honesty, and a reawakening of one's self-awareness. These steps are essential in ensuring that each party involved is on the same wavelength, preventing any undue suffering or hurt.

Ethical Non-monogamy

Multiple love affairs conducted with the full acceptance and assent of everyone entailed constitutes ethical non-monogamy. Involving practices such as open unions, polyamorous bonds, or swinger lifestyles, responsibly conducting these alliances mandates transparent communication, setting limits, and prioritizing the welfare and enthusiastic permission of all participants. Teach your kids about all these different relationships.

DISCUSSING HEALTHY FRIENDSHIPS AND BOUNDARIES

Friendships contribute significantly to our lives, influencing our relationships and helping us grow as individuals. As parents, it is imperative that we teach our kids how to form strong, healthy bonds and set limits appropriately. Discover ways to encourage your youngsters to build affirming connections and get familiarized with boundary-setting techniques that prioritize their wellness. Empower them toward flourishing interpersonal relationships by initiating friendly conversations and offering counsel. Here, we delve into approaches for congenially addressing vital aspects of friendship and restrictions with our dear ones.

Understanding Healthy Friendships

- **Mutual respect and support:** Encourage your children to appreciate the value of mutual respect and support among friends. Instruct them that wholesome companionship entails demonstrating affection, understanding, and consideration toward one another. With these elements in place, your child will begin to foster enduring connections built on admiration and assistance.

- **Shared interests and values:** Guide your child in seeking out friendship with peers who have similar passions, beliefs, and objectives. Establishing shared interests serves as an effective foundation for sturdy attachments that endure the test of time.
- **Trust and loyalty:** Stress the relevance of honesty and loyalty when forming friendships. Teach your child the merits of being devoted, truthful, and steadfast, and urge them to engage only with those who display these virtues. These principles lay the bedrock for long-lasting, rewarding associations.

Establishing Boundaries

- **Self-awareness:** Cultivate your child's self-awareness of their internal landscape by guiding them through the exploration of personal preferences, moral convictions, and threshold limitations across varying communal settings. By equipping them with insights into their innermost selves, they become capable of forming more genuine and meaningful relationships.

- **Communicating boundaries:** Educate your precious children on how to voice their boundaries assertively and respectfully. Tell them to make use of *I* declarations and clearly articulate their desires and limitations to their peers.

- **Recognizing and respecting others' boundaries:** Nurture in your child a profound understadning of the significance of establishing boundaries—both in drawing the line for themselves and in acknowledging the boundaries of others. Encourage them through discussions on the pivotal role that empathic listening and response play in their friendships. This enables them to learn how respecting their friends' boundaries with empathy and compassion establishes a lasting intimacy that fosters healthy and enriching relationships.

Navigating Conflict

- **Conflict resolution:** Empower your kid with the necessary skill set to handle conflicts between friends by equipping them with effective conflict resolution strategies. Instill in them the mindset of active listening, empathy, and transparent communication, which can lead to finding mutually enriching solutions and restoring unyielding peace within their friendships.
- **Encouraging autonomy:** Support your child in developing autonomy to discover what works best for them. Nurture independent decision-making skills so confidence blossoms in their own abilities and judgments.

Promoting Positive Online Friendships

- **Digital etiquette:** Unleash your child's digital potential by enlightening them on the essence of exhibiting responsible online conduct and treating individuals with tenderness and dignity. Explore the far-reaching ramifications of digital behavior and the indispensability of preserving online confidentiality and security.

- **Critical thinking:** Nurture your child's critical thinking by inspiring them to assess their virtual companions and to be aware of the details they share. Empower them to distinguish the hallmarks of healthy digital connections, voice their apprehensions, and report any unacceptable behavior.
- **Balancing online and offline friendships:** Foster equilibrium in your child's life by nurturing their ability to balance their virtual and physical world relationships. Propel them to cherish in-person interactions and endeavors that amplify social bonding and foster connection beyond the online sphere.

Supportive and Reassuring Approach

- **Active listening:** Lend your ear to your child's perspectives, fears, and queries on friendships and limitations with undivided attention. Demonstrate compassion and acknowledge their emotions, creating a nurturing atmosphere that is understanding and noncritical.
- **Role modeling:** Champion robust interpersonal associations and healthy limits in your personal entanglements. Exert a positive

impact as an exemplar by defining your boundaries articulately and communicating them effectively, setting an example worthy of emulation.

- **Encourage self-reflection:** Unleash your child's reflective prowess by engaging them to contemplate upon their own encounters, principles, and sentiments entwined with the notion of friends and limits. Allow them to embrace the idea that it's perfectly alright to reassess and realign their boundaries as they evolve and advance in life.

ADDRESSING ROMANTIC FEELINGS AND CRUSHES

As our young ones journey through the labyrinth of social interactions, they may encounter romantic feelings and experience a rush of crush. Nurturing a safe space for them to freely express their feelings and guiding them through the unchartered waters of romantic experiences is indispensable for parents. Here, we embark on a quest to unveil the ways to address and tackle these emotions with our children in an empowering and comforting manner. Through promoting unrestricted communication, empathy, and companionship, we pave the way for our little ones to steer through their emotional voyage and foster salubrious relationship practices.

Chatting About Childhood Crushes

Emit a vibe where your child feels confident to bear their soul and share their pearls of perception without hesitation. Embolden lighthearted dialogues about childhood crushes, granting them the freedom to articulate their emotions without criticism. Validate their emotions by exalting their experiences as typical and normal. Transmit their way a message that cherishing a crush is a natural milestone in the process of blooming and that countless have traversed on the same path.

Talking About Feelings

Inspire your child to unreservedly disclose their feelings. Create chances for them to talk about their feelings and lend a patient ear without evaluation or disruption. Instill in your child the conviction that their emotions hold importance and are authentic. Accommodate the force of their emotions while extending enlightenment and assurance in parallel.

Determining if the Crush is Mutual

Empower your child to ponder upon their crush's interest and reflect on their interactions as well. Engrain in them that a profound understanding, harmonious interests, and reciprocated feelings are the building blocks of a healthy romantic relationship. Delve into the realm of possibilities that the crush may not be reciprocated and guide them to perceive it as a natural outcome. Assure your little one that not all crushes culminate into a romantic liaison and it's common for them to undergo changes in their feelings during the course of their growth.

Discussing Appropriate Interactions

Inculcate the significance of prizing one's personal space and seeking consent before proceeding with any action. Assist your kid in differentiating between cordial interactions and behavior that might inflict discomfort on someone. Reinforce the significance of fostering a foundation of amity and acquaintanceship besides cherishing romantic emotions. Explore with them the pertinence of nurturing meaningful bonds that stem from shared interests, high regard, and empathy for one another.

Healing Hurt Feelings

In the event of your child facing rejection or disappointment, extend your unwavering support and listen to them. Acknowledge their emotions and motivate them to deliberate on their sentiments in healthy ways. Contribute toward having them comprehend that the culmination of their crush doesn't hold the key to self-assessment and worth. Promote the idea of channeling their energy toward personal growth, discovering uncharted territories, and nurturing robust bonds of amity with peers.

NAVIGATING PEER PRESSURE

As little ones advance and wander through their social spheres, they might confront diverse degrees of peer influence. Thus, it becomes paramount for us parents to provide our children with the savoir-faire and steering necessary tools to steer clear of negative peer pressure gracefully. In this discussion, we are unearthing tactics to handle peer pressure tactfully and endowing our kids with the ability to make shrewd decisions that comply with their beliefs and fitness. Fostering transparent communication, active engagement, and amplifying confidence enables us to help our young ones maneuver peer pressure with unwavering determination and self-assuredness.

Be Involved in Your Child's Life

Delve deep into your child's companionships and acquaint yourself with their social circle. Kindle their social interests and ensure that they are spending time with constructive influences. Remain actively involved in your child's hobbies and undertakings. By being there and participating, you can gain an insightful understanding of their social exchanges and lead the way when necessary.

Teach Them to Say "No"

Foster your child's ability to assert themselves by cultivating the confidence to voice their thoughts, establish boundaries, and say "no" when confronted with peer pressure. Through role-play simulations and practical guidance, equip them with the ability to tackle arduous situations. Inculcate in them the art of discernment and the power of independent decision-making, grounded in their beliefs, rather than giving in to the enticement of others. Instil in them the belief to place trust in their gut instincts and to have faith in their ethical compass.

Set Clear Family Rules and Stick to Them

Generate clear family rules and expectations that are in sync with your core principles. Examine these norms in an open forum with your children, clarifying the reason behind them. Uphold these family provisions assiduously and ensure their compliance with healthy consequences in the event of a violation. This steadfastness will reinforce a sense of orderliness for your child, thus fostering a crystal-clear understanding of the boundaries and fortifications in place.

Build Self-Esteem

Instill a positive self-image by placing the spotlight on your child's forte, capabilities, and exceptional attributes. Embolden them to recognize the beauty in their singularity and expand a wholesome sense of self. Compliment and commemorate your child's outstanding achievements, no matter how modest they may seem. Positive reinforcement boosts self-assurance and fortitude, thereby fortifying the child's poise and resistance to peer pressure.

Address Bullying

Nurture your child's graciousness and benevolence in their interactions with others. Impart the significance of countering bullying and being a compassionate friend. Construct a secure environment for your child, wherein they are at ease reporting instances of bullying. Teach them to reach out to responsible adults, be they teachers or school counselors in need of assistance.

Balance Independence and Supervision

Encourage gradual, age-appropriate strides toward independence, ensuring holistic yet regulated supervision. Gradual freedom bolsters their ability to make decisions and build self-assurance. Uphold an open dialogue with your child, delving deep into their experiences, apprehensions, and predicaments related to shared social influences. In addition to cultivating a sense of camaraderie, offer counsel and encouragement in moments of need.

BUILD LOVE, TRUST, AND COMMUNICATION WITH YOUR KID

Transforming a child-parent relationship into a flourishing and robust bond necessitates the construction of three essential pillars: love, trust, and effective communication. Once these pillars are instituted with ardor and sincerity, they create a nurturing ambiance that amplifies your child's sense of security and worth. This enriching topic will embark on a journey of unveiling strategies that enable you to cultivate and harvest each of these pillars into a thriving parent-child relationship, helping you to an unbreakable bond with your child, a bond that will positively steer their overall growth and well-being.

- **Show unconditional love:** Overflowing with unconditional love, let your child feel the depth of your affection, rooting for them at every step, irrespective of their accomplishments or conduct. Embrace them with open arms, accepting them for who they are, standing by them, and lending a hand of support at every turn through the ups and downs of life.

- **Spend quality time together:** Carve out a special time in your schedule, one that is exclusively dedicated to one-on-one interactions with your child. Engage in activities that tune into their unique interests and fascinations, weaving a tapestry of unforgettable moments. These moments of quality time constitute the fabric that stitches and reinforces your bond, opening avenues of honest communication that would otherwise remain close.

- **Be empathetic:** Empathy is the cornerstone of trust and understanding, an integral ingredient in the recipe for healthy relationships. To foster such a bond, one must embark on a journey of emotional empathy, stepping into the shoes of your child and validating their experiences, concerns, and feelings. Acknowledge their struggles without any judgment or dismissals, and watch the seeds of a deeper connection take root.

- **Respect their perspective:** Show reverence for your little one's thoughts and viewpoints, notwithstanding if they vary from your own.

Urge them to express their concepts, instilling a sense of independence and recognition.

- **Set clear boundaries:** Set up boundaries that are suitable for your child's age, offering a framework for support while still honoring their independence. Convey the reasoning behind these limits openly, emphasizing the significance of their welfare and security.
- **Consistency and trustworthiness:** Infuse your actions and words with the power of reliability and consistency that inspires trust within your child's heart. Let them rest assured that every commitment and promise you make shall be fulfilled with fidelity. Forging trust between parent and child necessitates unwavering honesty and steadfast dependability that you must always strive to cultivate.
- **Practice positive discipline:** Adopt disciplined tactics rooted in positivity that build a strong foundation for teaching, guidance, and forming healthy boundaries for your child, as opposed to punishment. Foster a growth mindset by recognizing and embracing the importance of learning from mistakes and cultivating personal growth. With every correction, take the opportunity to instill values that abide by the principles of respect and understanding.

- **Express appreciation and praise:** Delve deep into your hearts and acknowledge the efforts, accomplishments, and commendable actions of your little ones. It would be delightful to shower them with tokens of recognition and sincere praise regularly, as it would uplift their spirits, boost their self-confidence, and fill their hearts with a sense of fulfillment.

- **Encourage independence and autonomy:** Help your child spread their wings by providing them with opportunities that are well suited for their age to make choices and take ownership of their actions. Boost their confidence and decision-making skills by urging them to extract learnings from their experiences and inspire them to develop their proficiency in problem-solving.

- **Support their passions and interests:** Nurture your child's inner spark by wholeheartedly investing yourself in their hobbies, passions, and aspirations. Exhibit unwavering support and encouragement toward their dreams, while showcasing your unwavering belief in their abilities and truly cherishing their distinctive interests.

UNDERSTANDING EMOTIONS AND EMOTIONAL WELL-BEING

How splendidly intricate is the fabric of humanity, woven with threads of emotions that color our perspective and interactions with the world? For parents, it's imperative to assist our little ones in comprehending and regulating their emotions for their cognitive prosperity and all-round development. Here, we will delve into methods to aid our children in understanding their emotional realm, promoting wellness, and fostering a spirit of resilience. Imbued with positivity and empathy, we will equip our children with the tools to traverse the complex labyrinth of emotions in positive and constructive ways.

- **Emotion identification:** Aid your children in forging a deeper understanding of their emotional spectrum by identifying and giving voice to their emotions. Utilize terminology that is suitable for their age to outline and explain dissimilar emotions and talk with them about occurrences that trigger particular feelings. By performing these actions, you'll assist your child in cultivating emotional acuity, honing their capacity to articulate their emotional responses and navigate challenging situations in a measured way.

- **Emotional regulation:** It is delightful to impart to your little ones skillful ways to control their emotions. Techniques such as deep breathing, mindfulness, penning their thoughts, or indulging in art as a therapeutic activity can act as a balm when they feel something is amiss. Nurturing and developing these strategies can provide them with a robust repertoire to navigate their emotions adroitly and obtain a sense of serenity in trying times.

- **Empathy and understanding:** Imbue your child with the gift of empathy by motivating them to contemplate the sentiments and viewpoints of others. Supporting them to comprehend that every individual perceives and feels things distinctly, thereby cultivating benevolence and empathy toward others.

- **Problem-solving skills:** Nurture your child with the expertise to solve complex problems during emotional turbulence. Bolster their problem-solving capabilities by instilling in them the skill to identify optimal solutions, ponder over the aftermath of their actions, and uncover constructive techniques to resolve conflicts peacefully.

- **Emotional expression:** Inculcate in your child the desire to exhibit their emotions in a healthy manner, for example, through creative crafts, journaling, or dialogues. Imbue in them the knowledge that expressing their emotions is a quintessential and intrinsic part of their emotional stability, helping them attain a sound state of mind.

- **Building resilience:** Motivate your children to build an unyielding spirit by instilling in them the practice of resilience in the face of hindrances and adversities. Foster a growth-oriented outlook that accentuates the fact that blunders and setbacks are openings for learning and evolution of the self. Through this, you can empower your child to acquire the skill of resilience, a key to thriving in life.

- **Encouraging self-care:** Enlighten your precious ones with the significance of self-care and place their well-being on top of the priority list. Embolden them to discover activities that kindle gratification, serenity, and revival, thereby nurturing a feeling of emotional wellness within. Through this, you can gift your child the art of cherishing themselves and upholding sound mental health, laying a strong foundation for a fulfilling life.

- **Seeking support when needed:** Nurture your children to confide in reliable individuals, be they their guardians, mentors, or advisors, when they require assistance in regulating their emotions or navigating complicated circumstances.

- **Cultivating gratitude:** Instill a precious attitude of gratefulness in your child's heart by directing their attention toward the delightful aspects of their life. Encourage them to contemplate the things they hold dear and appreciate, fostering an optimistic outlook and promoting emotional well-being for your little one.

- **Promoting a balanced lifestyle:** By encouraging them to develop healthy habits that encompass essential components such as plentiful rest, nourishing meals, regular physical exertion, and ample opportunities for unwinding and enjoying leisure activities. It's your role as a caregiver to promote and support these balanced practices, setting the foundation for a vibrant and fulfilling existence for your child.

DISCUSSING HEALTHY COPING MECHANISMS AND STRESS MANAGEMENT

Life is like a wilderness of obstacles and stressors, and our children must have the aptitude to navigate through the thickets. As caring parents, we are bestowed with the responsibility to guide our children toward the light with effective stress management strategies. This section delves into the various healthy coping approaches and stress management techniques that can empower our future generation to take control of their stress effectively and constructively. We are going to explore activities such as creativity, social backing, and relaxation while encouraging a decisive mindset shift toward active coping. We can enable the molding of the resilient character of our kids and promote their all-around well-being in the long run.

Active Coping Strategies

Empower your child with the skills to confront challenges by teaching them how to break them down into smaller, manageable steps. Urge them to weave possible solutions into actionable plans, taking one step at a time while injecting zeal into their efforts. Teach your child how to manage their time productively by laying emphasis on prioritization, enabling realistic goal-setting, and preserving an ideal school-life balance.

Regular exercise is a tried-and-true strategy to help your child feel better overall, lower stress levels, and improve their well-being. Encourage them to embrace physical activity as an active stress management tool and watch them flourish in every sector of their lives.

Relaxing Coping Strategies

- **Deep breathing exercises:** Introduce your child to the art of deep breathing techniques, such as diaphragmatic breathing or box breathing, as a calming mechanism to ease their minds and bodies amid times of distress.
- **Progressive muscle relaxation:** Take your child on an exciting journey of progressive muscle relaxation exercises, where they can relax and refresh both their minds and bodies in an orderly fashion by systematically tightening and loosening various muscle groups. Relish in the experience of promoting relaxation, ridding of any tension or burden your child may be experiencing with this invigorating approach.
- **Mindfulness and meditation:** Open your child's world to the wonders of mindfulness and meditation, guiding them toward developing a profound sense of mindfulness and tranquility in the present moment.

Creative Coping Strategies

- **Art therapy:** Inspire your child to unleash their feelings and ideas through the captivating realm of art, be it by sketching, portraying with colors, or chiseling. Feeding their passion for artistic expression can supply a potent release for pent-up emotions and stress.
- **Writing or journaling:** Help your kid discover self-reflection and expression via writing journals! The therapeutic journey will allow them to sort through, comprehend, and communicate emotional experiences so their inner light keeps glowing brighter!
- **Engaging in hobbies:** Encourage your child's creativity and passion by nurturing beloved hobbies such as music-making, movement arts, and craftsmanship. Embrace joyful diversions while reducing stress through fun personal pursuits!

Social Coping Strategy

Another aspect of a healthy coping mechanism involves fostering strong interpersonal connections with others —whether family, friends, or neighbors. Encouraging interactions within the home environment should, therefore, come naturally for those raised therein;

however, allowing youngsters the freedom to interact socially outside the safety net provided at home requires trust and preparation on behalf of us as guardians. When ready, permit your child to partake in group discussions that are rich with purpose, where they can truly express themselves with like-minded peers. These moments will serve as important milestones along their path toward personal growth and happiness, not only providing solace but also memories shared together over many years ahead.

Coping Strategies That Shift Mindset

- **Positive affirmations:** Guide your children to cultivate uplifting self-talk and powerful affirmations. Join forces in transforming negatives into radiant positives and watch confidence flourish before your very eyes!
- **Reframing:** Assist your child in shifting their perspective toward difficult circumstances by motivating them to explore alternative viewpoints and concentrate on potential solutions or opportunities for personal development.
- **Gratitude practice:** Nurture a deep sense of thankfulness in your children by inspiring them to recognize and cherish the good qualities of their lives. Practicing gratitude can aid in

transforming their mindset toward a more optimistic and hopeful outlook on life.

ENCOURAGING OPEN COMMUNICATION WITHIN THE FAMILY

A family flourishes when communication flows freely and effectively, forming an unshakable foundation that ties its members together. By fostering a safe space where each individual is encouraged to share their ideas, feelings, and apprehensions, family bonds deepen, trust and empathy are built, and a sense of togetherness blossoms. In this section, we will delve into approaches that fuel transparent communication within families, cultivate robust relations, resolve disagreements productively, and erect an ambiance of kindness and love.

Schedule Family Time

Create a schedule that accommodates each member's availability and gives paramount importance to this cherished time as an avenue for transparent communication and strengthened family ties. Immerse yourself in activities that facilitate captivating conversations and harmonious bonding—be it engaging games, refreshing walks, or indulging in shared passions.

Eat Meals Together

Bring your loved ones together regularly for nurturing meals and enjoy quality time as a cohesive unit. Savor moments filled with purposeful conversations, lively sharing, and undivided attention. Banish distractions by making dinnertime a device-less oasis where relations grow stronger and warm memories emerge.

Be an Active Listener

Embrace mindful listening within the family. Offer complete concentration to those sharing their thoughts while holding their gaze and steering clear of disrupting them. Encourage each family member to express with sincerity and assurance no one shall be suppressed or belittled. Verbalize acceptance of individual feelings and promote emotional comprehension through validation.

Show Kindness and Appreciation

Create a tapestry of warmth and compassion within the family. Let's sprinkle the magic of gratitude for each other's efforts and contributions. Inspire every member to speak kind words, shower compliments, and celebrate each other's strengths and exceptional traits. Such a nurturing environment not only blossoms with positivity but also creates a resilient support system that helps in overcoming challenges.

Establish Family Routines

Forge unchanging family routines that unlock channels for communication. Consider orchestrating customary family gatherings or rendezvous, where each individual can articulate their musings and anxieties or exchange news. By establishing routines, you engender a feeling of constancy and reliability, thereby facilitating family members to reveal themselves more comfortably.

Allow for One-on-One Time

Nurture a deeper connection between family members by prioritizing one-on-one time. This creates a cozy, confidential setting in which intimate conversations can unfold without any distractions. Plan unique excursions or engagements that allow each family member to bond and share in an unhurried and mindful ambiance. Such individual attention bolsters the relations that bind and enhances mutual comprehension, leading to stronger bonds.

Attack the Problem, Not Each Other

Amid the storm of conflicts, focus on finding a way out of the tempest instead of pointing fingers. Train your child to convey their misgivings with grace, lend a compassionate ear, and rally together to find feasible answers. Foster compassion, embrace the art of give-

and-take, and discover shared areas of understanding and agreement.

Stay Connected

In this incredible era of constant hustle, it's crucial to stay in touch with your beloved family members. Maximize technology's potential by utilizing video conferencing and messaging applications to keep in touch with family members who may not be residing under the same roof. Keep a regular check on each other's well-being, share the latest tidbits, and don't hesitate to express your profound care and support.

5

MEDIA LITERACY AND ONLINE SAFETY

Knowing all about phones, computers, and electronic gadgets can be challenging. Be ready to handle any problems because kids often copy us adults. We should be smart web users, too, so we teach them well. Don't just assume they automatically get it or that schools cover everything (not always true!) This takes effort from you but it pays off... and keeps your home life calmer!

The power of videos, pictures, and words is huge for growing minds! Young brains copy, watch, and read stuff easily, so choose the media carefully. Let's get smarter ourselves first, then advise them. This chapter tells you how to pick top media for good examples; explain what's real and imaginary; help your kid figure out tricks; and set limits for time spent staring at tiny screens. They benefit later, trust me, plus peace reigns again at home once the routine is fixed. Learning media and internet wisdom lets kids act smarter. Discovering the truth amid deceptive adverts and unreal pictures needs clever detectives nowadays. This chapter shares tips to raise young viewers, like finding reliable people to follow online, and books worth borrowing. Arming youthful brains means fewer mix-ups in the future since their gullible eyes take cues from what you show them regularly. So explore here alone and gain insight; young minds depend on your media mindfulness!

Being safe online matters—teach your kids privacy rules, too. Show them bad internet folk and how to avoid viruses. Learn tricks to spot fakes to prevent being conned. Prepare young minds properly before letting them go to the virtual Wild West alone. Plus, bonus fun ideas sprinkled throughout for screen breaks without boredom blues after heavy device play. Enjoy learning ahead with those little ones and grownups alike!

Real-world experience shows screens aren't bad for families—until misused. Smart habits strengthen relationships built upon respect and honesty, starting with transparent parent talk. Mindful rules nurture positive digital experiences and promote a clear vision for balanced tech usage. Appreciating how beneficial online resources can broaden horizons encourages everyone's participation when using gadgets, rather than alienation due to fear tactics.

TEACHING CRITICAL MEDIA LITERACY SKILLS

Let's face facts: Screens dominate our culture. To give our kids a fair chance at being savvy citizens in a tech world, we need to teach them smart strategies early on. Media literacy isn't about banning electronics but training little eyes to spot biased news reports or fake stories. It's shaping their web search habits even before typing Google questions with tiny hands. The next generation deserves our efforts to arm them against scams and misleading info—that's why learning media wisdom is vital for your family. With each new skill acquired, they'll grow more self-reliant without relying solely on grownup help!

Understanding the Power of Media

Explaining media stuff starts here with identifying its sway on society and behaviors. Examine various types with curious minds like TV, video games, social sites, and so on. Discuss motives driving mass messages; consider implications of blind approval. Help kids see connections so they critique ads and articles smarter. Open dialogues lead children into deepening scrutiny about why media exists and affects all ages. These talks prepare families to evaluate both good and problematic facets of media influence.

Developing Analytical Thinking

Urge them to enquire about things, look at presuppositions, and gather different perspectives when they consume media content. Help them figure out which sources are dependable, examine facts, and ascertain any logical misunderstandings. Get involved in conversations regarding how the media depicts circumstances and people, assisting them in acquiring a scrutinizing viewpoint. Through encouraging interest and doubt, you're supporting their capacity for autonomous choice-making.

Spotting Fake News and Misinformation

In today's world, it's easy for kids to get lost in all the online info out there. But learning how to tell real stuff from made-up nonsense is important. Here's some advice on how to teach your little ones to do that: Firstly, have them double-check things they read. They can look at multiple sources and compare notes (kind of like how detectives solve crimes). Also, check if sites sound trustworthy—if it sounds fishy, it probably is. Finally, remind them to ask questions if something seems off or exaggerated; oftentimes, these are just trying to trick readers into thinking one thing happened when actually something else did.

Media Literacy in the Age of Social Media

Social media has become huge these days. Kids need some guidance on using it, though, because it's got both good and bad aspects. It's essential to guide them as parents on how to use it well without getting taken advantage of, acting rudely, or accidentally revealing private stuff. Show them how to think about the risks involved with what gets posted online—even pics can lead to bullies targeting folks or causing harm (and sometimes it isn't just harmless fun either)... basically, guide your kid on being savvy netizens who act responsibly in virtual spaces.

TEACH THE PORTRAYAL OF SEX AND RELATIONSHIPS IN MEDIA

Dealing with sexuality in the media can get tricky for both adults and kids alike. However, as caretakers, it's essential that we arm ourselves and our children with the necessary tools to navigate this minefield. The goal here is to promote a positive perspective on intimacy, consent, and healthy relationships. To achieve this aim, sit down with your children and discuss their thoughts regarding such matters while presenting other views;

this should foster enlightening discourse and enable wise decisions. This topic will provide you with practical strategies to effectively teach your kids about the portrayal of sex and relationships in the media.

Identify Problematic Behaviors

When discussing sex and relationships in the media, begin by getting your kids' input. Ask them what they've witnessed or picked up from different channels. Encouraging them to speak freely allows room for sharing their points of view, which sets up an environment conducive to chatting and correcting incorrect perceptions.

Encourage Critical Viewing

Teach your kids how to critically evaluate portrayals of sex and relationships in media content. Urge them to ask questions, dig into messages, and gauge potential impacts on genuine connections. Help them pick out distorted situations, cliches, and overemphasized displays. Instructing them in judgment skills assists in making educated selections and distinguishing truth from fiction.

Distinguish Between Healthy and Unhealthy Portrayals

Talk to your kids about determining healthier versus unhealthy portrayals of sex and relationship conduct. Discuss with them notions of consensus, correspondence, and regard inside connections. Train them to spot warning signs of unhealthy dynamic qualities, such as pressure tactics, deficiency of permission, or disregard. Providing them with a structure for comprehending healthier relations arms them with implements to form gratifying connections grounded in reciprocal admiration and trust.

Encouraging Critical Analysis of Media Messages

The best way to educate children about sexual matters is to get them to examine and analyze media messages, focusing on intentions, economic drives, and ad campaigning... and then challenge stereotypes and objectification. This trains them to interact with media material thoughtfully and select their own consumption wisely. Make sure to promote investigative competencies so they can be mindful choosers of media articles.

Addressing Sexualization and Objectification

Sexualization and objectification are prevalent in media portrayals. Speak to your children about possible results upon self-worthiness, physicality judgments, and bonds in close personal connections—and also underscore the significance of esteem and fair-mindedness for each person and themselves. Focus on well-grounded appreciation of consent and boundaries. All this readies children to create healthy perspectives about physiques and relationships.

Talk about the Positive and Negative Aspects

It is important to show both the positive and negative parts of how the mass media addresses topics related to love and sex... so our children acquire a more rounded viewpoint to utilize when taking in information. Having these kinds of chats means we raise awareness around wholesome and lifelike media presentations, along with instances where harmful stereotypes or behaviors are perpetuated. Help your kids gain a sharper outlook by showing them various levels of media portrayals. By doing this, they will come to understand and judge media representations better.

Provide Alternative Media

Become their guide toward suitable resources that contain constructive and truthful accounts of romantic links and unions. Show them age-appropriate books, movies, and TV programs that feature various types of relationships based on mutual agreement, chat, and empathy. Providing them with many sides makes it simpler for them to know all the different kinds of bonds and sets great examples. Your decisions play a major role in establishing their outlooks and ethics!

ADDRESSING THE INFLUENCE OF PORNOGRAPHY AND ITS UNREALISTIC EXPECTATIONS

In our current technological era, where pornographic material is effortlessly accessible, parents must handle this issue together with their little ones. Since you're a dependable mentor, take advantage of your possibilities to talk about the impact of such material and its fantasized prospects for genuine partnerships. You should concentrate on instructing them about the variations between adult amusement in magazines or online and actual-life emotional closeness. Explain safety features and appropriate ages for watching certain stuff. Initiating these sorts of talks gives you a chance to provide them with useful techniques to deal with the subject matter of online pornography and aid them in shaping well-founded feelings pertaining to intercourse and relationships.

Explain the Difference Between Pornography and Real-Life Intimacy

One thing you could do to address the effect of pornography on children is to help them distinguish what's authentic from what's fake. Stress that erotic materials aren't always honest reproductions of real-life couplings—those typically don't get shown publicly because they wouldn't be allowed due to censorship rules. In reality, human interactions involving passion include consent, sincerity, and being tender, which shouldn't be equated only with pleasure, but rather overall fondness and respect.

Explain the Role of Media Filters and Age Restrictions

Talk to your kids regarding media filters and age limits to safeguard them from grown-up content material. Make clear that these procedures exist so that they stay safe and feel comfortable while browsing the net and viewing articles and videos. In case your kids stumble upon improper articles or discover anything distressing, motivate them to turn to you for assistance and advice.

Discuss Real Intimacies Vs. Fantasized Ones

Carry out honest dialogues relating to reality-based intimacies and assist your children in distinguishing between fantasized experiences presented through porno images and real-life intimate relationships founded upon emotional connection, trust, and communication. Develop an ambiance permitting them to query freely and share their ideas as well as sensations.

Explain Unrealistic Expectations Presented in Pornography

Talk over misguided beliefs created by video clips of pornography that do not showcase actual people's experiences, emphasizing that performers and scenes are regularly arranged, which means they don't signify the range of authentic life physical activities. Remind them body designs vary and true approval, harmonious regard, and interaction are indispensable within sexually committed alliances.

Sexualized Thinking

Speak about sexualized thinking generated due to the sight of sexually charged imagery. Make plain that gazing at explicit portraits could cause incorrect prejudices concerning usual or anticipated scenarios in genuine living settings. Inspire them to think rationally when it comes to mass media messages and reject exploitation or undesirable perspectives about women or men.

Discuss Addiction

Talk to your children about the potentially hazardous impacts of being addicted to pornographic materials. Reveal they must guard against letting this kind of substance rule other aspects of their daily lives, which might endanger partnerships, personal convictions, and joy; in case they find themselves trying to restrain their utilization, persuade them to look for professional support.

Monitor Their Internet Usage

You should take responsibility as a parent to maintain an eye on your little ones' web utilization. Install suitable controls as parents and define regulations pertaining to how they should behave whenever online. Have continuous discussions regarding their cyber adventures and provide counseling along with backing each time essential. Formulate an environment of sincerity and openness, allowing them to reveal any troubles or worries they might possess.

Educating About Online Safety and Privacy

Online exchanges play a significant role in most people's lifestyles these days. It's vital to enlighten our children about safe practices with regard to web security and discretion. As their mothers and fathers as well as keepers, it falls directly into our own hands to supply them with the awareness and skills required to get around the virtual planet safeguarded and assured. Through coaching these individuals pertaining to risks such as bad guys, bullies online, ripoffs, and additional difficulties linked to net utilization, as well as fixing principles for their actions via the World Wide Web, we will inspire them all to build intelligent judgments as well as safeguard their particular details.

Teach Them the Potential Risks

Teach them there might be hazards on digital platforms like identity thievery, hoaxes, and contact with wrong matters. Advise them to stay alert when using network services and guard their private details. Guide them into being mindful of possible results caused by revealing personal details or clicking strange links and attachments. The sooner they learn to act cautiously online, the safer they will remain browsing sites and social applications.

Educate Them About Online Safety and Privacy

Instruct your children regarding the appropriate use of code words and ways to select and change security setups to manage others seeing stuff posted online. Help comprehend why it is necessary for security password protection to stop unauthorized users and dishonest entities. Show ways to identify safe web addresses and avoid tricky emails attempting to extract sensitive facts for nefarious purposes.

Teach Them About Online Predators

Educate them about internet stalkers and the need to stay vigilant throughout conversations with unknown contacts from net space. Warn them to prevent exchanging personal material, including images and location info, unless they are sure about their identities. Stress children to turn to trusted elders whenever they face dubious happenings in chat rooms or run into someone behaving oddly toward them. Always keep them up-to-date with basic measures of internet safety so they can make smart choices in the future!

Talk About Cyberbullying

Talk about cyberbullying found over networks, which can ruin somebody's state of mind and emotions, and how hurtful words could lead to despair and unease. Teach children the values of kindness and esteem instead of ridiculing or mistreating friends online. Urge kids not to neglect seeking assistance during times of harassment experienced personally or observed in communication apps used between friends or classmates.

Teach Them About Online Scams

Guide children around artificial scams appearing on online platforms that attempt to cheat users out of money or valuable data. Describe popular methods employed by rogues like impostor email messages, deceitful websites imitating reputable companies, or appeals trying to get hold of sensitive particulars. Guideline them to look at each proposal doubtfully and never hurry straight into handing over a credit card or personal secrets without doing some research first.

Set Standards for What Your Kids Can and Cannot Do Online

Make guidelines and limitations concerning kids' usage of technology and online activity in order to help maintain healthy habits and appropriate conduct. Limit hours spent engaged with devices and screens, and specify acceptable materials to view. Set boundaries regulating what can and cannot be viewed via browsers and social media apps.

Encourage Them to Come to You If They Encounter a Problem

Build a warm and welcoming ambiance, allowing children to turn to you when facing complications or nervousness due to digital experiences. Convince them there won't be negative feedback for coming to you but rather empathy plus aid by setting good rapport through effective interaction strengthened by mutual reliance. Create a harmonious bond through understanding and dependable connection where both parties benefit from clear talk when required!

Use a Kid-Friendly Search Engine

Guide children to select child-orientated versions of online search tools designed to obstruct explicit or other unwanted articles to guarantee safe browsing adventures full of learning chances sans distressing encounters with undesirable substances. Promote the utilization of such sources when carrying out investigations or checking fresh topics for additional security during sessions!

Recognizing the Potential Risks of Sexting and Cyberbullying

In today's modern era, as technology plays a big role in our everyday lives, it's crucial to teach ourselves, along with our children, the dangers linked with sexting and cyberbullying. These involve sending lewd pics, texts, or videos, as well as mistreating folks using technology, causing worry or fear. As parents and grown-ups, comprehending these threats lets us prepare our progeny to act sensibly and appropriately online, thus averting troubled moments and protecting them from lawful penalties. Look here to learn helpful knowledge that assists one during stressful situations, bolsters confidence, and takes positive steps moving forward together!

Understanding Sexting

Start by making sure your children know exactly how sexting works and its potential drawbacks; don't forget to emphasize that once they share explicit content, they lose control over it and how quickly such images get passed around, and it becomes difficult to retrieve them back like lost property. Have frank conversations on respectful partnerships, approval, plus detrimental outcomes on mental state and potential legal actions resulting from getting tangled up in sexting.

Recognizing the Risks of Sexting

Teach yourself and your kids about the troubles related to sexting; explain cases of situations spreading without authorization, being used against someone as payback or blackmail. Realize how sensitive posts could remain and influence people negatively for a long time—so keep such interactions amongst mature counterparts only! Whenever necessary, refresh yourself first, then convey useful advice.

Understanding Cyberbullying

Talk things over with your children concerning cyber-bullying and ways to stop any negative vibes via tech methods like messaging apps or social sites; show them the differences between playful joking and malevolent treatment or intimidation. Make clear that victims aren't always aware of the perpetrator's identity due to the virtual nature of the attack; therefore, preventative measures must stay vigilant on both sides of the interaction.

Recognizing the Signs of Cyberbullying

Speak with your little ones on understanding symptoms of cyberbullying; urge them to observe alterations like increased sadness, apprehension when using technology, or disinterest in typically enjoyed hobbies. Impress them to bring to light discovered misconduct through trustworthy elders or faculty staff and always seek guidance whenever needed; rest assured your kid won't have to face this alone.

Promoting Positive Online Behavior

Train your children in practicing positive digital habits featuring warmth, regard, and courtesy; coach them to contemplate responses prior to posting online, considering others' sentiments, too. Instruct them on the merit of standing up on behalf of bullied peers; help create a safer network sphere!

Developing Digital Resilience

Give kids tools allowing them to tackle distressing internet occurrences; advise approaches strengthening mental toughness and personal worthiness alongside constructive problem-solving strategies. Advise them to ask for additional backing from reliable figures should uncomfortable events arise; ensure access to seasoned counsel also.

Empowering Bystanders

Empower youngsters to join forces standing against hurtful habits in the online world; embolden empathetic intervention where required; educate them on suitable courses of action should unacceptable activities surface, like telling grownups who manage relevant issues arena. By doing all the above, we collectively inspire an ethical mindset that carries into future interactions.

NAVIGATING SOCIAL MEDIA AND HEALTHY DIGITAL HABITS

Social media is everywhere these days! People use it to stay connected, share things they care about, and learn new stuff. But since kids might not have the same perspective as adults, it's up to you, grown-ups, to make sure they use it safely and wisely. Teach them how to act online so nothing bad happens (like talking to strangers who aren't actually nice). Set some rules around screen time so phones don't take over their free time. Show examples of what makes a great post vs. one that would embarrass them later. And also, share your own experiences—good and bad—so they know why following certain guidelines matters. Together, by taking these steps and making sure the little ones benefit from the cool parts of social media, they'll grow into thoughtful young adults ready to rock whatever comes next!

Understanding the Benefits and Challenges of Social Media

Talk with your children about the benefits and challenges of using social media platforms. Highlight chances to connect with friends and family far away or connect with users who share similar hobbies. Discover fun ways to create unique ideas and present talents not usually displayed in public. Nonetheless, there are factors like poor self-image, risk of addiction, loss of privacy, or setting limits on smartphone usage. Keep the conversation casual but insightful!

Fostering Digital Well-being

Foster your child's overall welfare while browsing the web by guiding them to conserve mental and emotional health through interactive websites. Direct them to spot early warning signals of digital burnout and make adjustments accordingly: take breaks and use mindful breathing. Nudge them to custom-pick online connections—pick accounts that boost positivity vs. choosing accounts that cause negative feelings and envy.

Practicing Mindful Social Media Use

Coach children's significance of mindful social media use. Guide them to monitor inner thoughts during net browsing and actively ask questions regarding content validity, including potential motives behind uploaded content! Nurture wise judgment whether information feels truthful or the intended purpose is unclear. These steps would help establish balanced virtual experiences based on facts instead of impulse decisions leading to incorrect conclusions or misinformation spread!

Promoting Positive Engagement

Promote positive engagement on social media platforms. Assist children in generating and contributing to internet spaces in beneficial manners. Motivate sharing joyous content, helpful tips, and supporting online communities. Instruct them about ethical internet actions: treating all web contacts kindly and thoughtfully and embracing variety among those we interact with in cyberspace!

Balancing Online and Offline Connections

Highlight appreciation for balancing both physical meetups and virtual hangouts. Urge kids to focus efforts equally toward preserving in-person relations where one gets direct eye contact and smiles! Remind them true friendship can grow through common offline interests done together, unlike solely relating virtually through posts and pictures viewed alone. The balance between these two forms of human bonding helps children enjoy many types of genuine friendships, which may lead to empathetic social abilities once adults!

Being Mindful of Digital Footprint

Help your children understand the concept of a digital imprint, making sure actions leave lasting impressions of intelligence and reliability. Explain how the accumulation of clicks leaves a trace in the long run. Educate children on considering what effects posting specific memories might have later on. Remind them it shapes how peers view them, plus opportunity doors open up depending on the online portfolio maintained!

ENCOURAGING RESPONSIBLE TECHNOLOGY USE AND DIGITAL CITIZENSHIP

As society advances through tech improvements, teaching our children responsible technology use and digital citizenship makes a big difference! We can optimize benefits using smart choices and staying safe online. In essence, becoming solid digital role models means setting shining examples so these new generations grow wiser and savvier than us... just like previous generations taught us crucial values.

Embrace the Benefits of Technology

Speak highly about the numerous benefits of technology and its positive impact. Illustrate examples such as chatting at ease across borders through messengers and video calls, possible now more than ever; easy retrieval and accessibility of information right when needed; and endless tools available for efficiency spikes! Encourage a positive outlook toward technology's ever-evolving nature, always bringing fresh advancements meant to improve society as a whole!

Model Responsible Technology Use

Become role models; practice what you preach when monitoring kids' excessive screen usage. Set reasonable limitations via routine screen breaks and family activities to ensure wholesome living! Leading such behaviors not only curbs child addiction issues but demonstrates mature digital choices for the entire household. This serves family unity, encouraging individual interests while still giving ample opportunity to experience various fun hobbies away from gadgets—leading a balanced lifestyle in this digitally interconnected globe.

Foster Positive Digital Citizenship

Emphasize the importance of being a responsible digital citizen. Guide your children to treat all individuals equally online, no matter how close one is living—next door or someone halfway across planet Earth. Help youth understand sharing bitter content will likely result in hurting feelings; encourage creating rather than destroying. Kids watching parents act maturely online could influence positive behaviors in the future!

Engage in Positive Online Activism

Foster the idea of using internet influence to make the world a better place! Inspire kids to bring change through sharing passions and concerns. Engage peers in discussing current events and consequences and express feelings about societal problems. Remind them to participate peacefully yet assertively, addressing improvements desired in this world.

PROMOTING A POSITIVE ONLINE PRESENCE AND RESPECTFUL BEHAVIOR

Show kids how to leave lasting, positive footprints on the World Wide Web equals to a better society! Become net citizens contributing to a friendlier online climate. The guidance includes strategies supporting diversity and creating accountable, reliable virtual relationships.

Teach Them to Be Mindful of Their Tone

Provide guidance around verbal choices made online. Educate children to not only focus on quantity but also on the quality of wording used when posting, commenting, and messaging. Respect toward fellow users helps create warm and kind vibes across the net community! Choosing words wisely helps keep disagreements in check while remaining productive in finding solutions to mutual concerns.

Tell Them to Be Aware of Their Audience

Guide children to have an understanding of audiences while publishing stuff digitally; recommend consideration before posting materials that certain language and content might upset some viewers. Be open to feedback from those you directly communicate with since their suggestions will help expand the content acceptance scope. The goal should be creating an inviting environment that feels welcoming to all kinds of folks regardless of any prejudice!

Ask Them to Be Themselves

Inspire kids to be original and genuine through online presence. Remind them to feel secure showcasing their specific tastes and interests, which truly reflects who they are, instead of imitating popular fads or comparing themselves to others. Their one-of-a-kind character traits bring something special to this world!

Help Them Be Forgiving

Cultivate forgiveness by advising children to graciously respond to others' online errors and mishaps. Provide room for learning without shutting down communication channels due to misunderstandings or disputes. Explain to children that everyone deserves chances at improvement rather than dwelling on past events that went wrong. Moments that initially seemed unfavorable can push growth!

Help Your Kids Develop a Thick Skin

Nurture resilience and a thick skin by helping them learn how to distinguish between helpful and disheartening messages. Instruct them to handle difficult situations online that could damage confidence levels in positive ways so that similar problems won't affect them later in life. When confronted by troublesome circumstances online, urge kids to reach out to nearby adult figures who believe in youth abilities and qualities —these allies assist during rough times until kiddos build self-assurance and inner strength via overcoming setbacks.

Follow What Would Grandma Say? (WWGS?) Rule

Train the WWGS? principle by helping children contemplate ahead before uploading content. Ask themselves, "How will the family react?" as a way to encourage polite behavior on socials like it's typical conduct in everyday living when interacting around close family members (grandparents). By applying this principle, youngsters may become more cautious when leaving comments online—taking the time to think beforehand instead of impulsively reacting to whims that sometimes turn out regrettably.

Don't Friend Strangers

Cutting back on stranger connections seems best since unknown users cannot always be relied on or hold honesty; thus, promote child safety online by encouraging only virtual friendships based upon actual links away from the screen. Let them focus on friends who they have met physically first prior to reaching out virtually. Kids must remain alert when new contacts come knocking because there'll probably be no guarantee of protection unless friendship is established through non-digital mediums first.

Be Patient Yourself

Be a role model and set good examples when using technology: act kindly, chat responsibly, discuss matters gracefully, and never ignore the power social media holds! Little eyes watch closely—make your actions worth copying for healthy and positive virtual lives ahead. Show the benefits of practicing patience while operating gadgets... their impression depends on your example!

Nurturing a beneficial online presence and promoting acceptable conduct will be necessary for acquiring a harmonious electronic local community. By training each of our little ones to be considerate and connected with other folks, being familiar with their spirits, being aware of their viewers, and even turning into themselves on their own, many of us equip them to successfully navigate the internet world with selflessness and proper care. Just by nourishing leniency, allowing out little ones to establish stamina, and demonstrating tenderness, many of us contribute to a confident electric environment. Collectively, this allows us to lead the subsequent era toward dependable electrical power citizenship, in which reverence, passion, and legitimacy prevail throughout almost all online dealings.

6

CONSENT, BOUNDARIES, AND HEALTHY RELATIONSHIPS

P arental guidance plays a crucial part in raising awareness regarding consent, boundaries, and harmonious interpersonal relationships for youngsters. Your role is to impart wisdom and experience from past encounters and the latest news reports. Explain what consent means (and why asking first before touching someone) sets safe and healthy standards! Identifying the right boundaries will benefit future decision-making (who to trust) and also set clear lines between friendly vs. flirtatious conduct in school or work settings. A healthy relationship foundation involves mutual understanding, respect, and compromise, plus good communication skills applied regularly. Open dialogue assists in cultivating mature and independent thinkers prepared to tackle societal issues later down the road!

Simply put, consent matters greatly both on personal and general levels. Acknowledging that permission must always be requested and given prior to taking action means better relationships! When people get consent education, learning to recognize respect builds a support system encouraging empathetic and caring attitudes throughout the community! Boundary setting keeps individuals secure, valued, and free to say "no thanks." Learning boundaries boosts children's confidence in declaring limits and owning space around themselves—whether alone or with friends or family members. Respectfully honoring boundaries in return strengthens inter-relational connections, thus improving the atmosphere! Just remember: Boundaries aren't meant to close doors but rather aim to keep spaces respected!

Building strong, positive peer connections early on teaches children several helpful traits. Raising socially skilled and emotionally intelligent children happens through parent-led guidance during budding friendships. Helping little ones understand and practice respectful engagement and listening techniques during fun times actually builds great habits, founding lifetime relationships with fuller joy! Kids who experience stable home routines get ready for happy outside adventures with new friends simply by having more knowledge shared via calm, relaxed talks with trustworthy adults. Applying simple examples means improved social skills acquired easily before entering stressful teen years!

DEFINING CONSENT AT DIFFERENT AGES

A simple thing to teach young minds about the important subject of consent is that it's an essential part of maintaining healthy relationships based on respect and effective communication. While nurturing growing human beings, help build blocks by establishing awareness early on and equipping your kid with the confidence to request permission before acting upon something. Begin during toddlerhood and progress as needed as your little one grows up to adolescence. Always keep the dialogue open and positive. By reinforcing these concepts frequently, we set good examples and cultivate solid relationships across generations.

What is Consent?

In simple language, explain what consent actually involves: Permission obtained willingly without pressure and fully comprehending consequences is a key point across ages. We must stress acknowledging others' choices, no matter their decision. Just because someone says yes does not mean yes forever, nor should it be assumed yes applies tomorrow or under different circumstances. It's our duty to communicate with kids so understanding goes hand in hand rather than confusion arising.

To Preschoolers

In the early stages, when your little one isn't familiarized with social norms such as physical space yet, start training them by introducing basic notions of setting private regions around the body: the personal space bubble and educating through playtime and storybooks that everyone possesses a unique private zone where only mommy and daddy are allowed to enter (for diaper changes, bathing, and feeding purposes). This initial exposure prepares the next step, which leads to discussing bodily autonomy, the absolute right of power held solely by oneself over one's own body choices. Make certain conversations are fun, easy, and visual to grasp by always using colorful illustrations. A strong foundation lays down stepping stones for continuation as they grow older, acquiring deeper knowledge and practice of asking permission ahead of time and accepting refusal gracefully.

To Elementary Schoolers

Speak to elementary schoolers regarding consent's significance and, where applicable, life circumstances. Explain the meaning behind listening when "no" is said and why it's significant. Demonstrate how it pertains in day-to-day situations using actual examples or scenarios! Emphasize the "stop" and "no" words as an option if anything doesn't feel right or one needs distance. Through games, storytelling makes comprehension simpler and aids retention as they progress in the years ahead!

To Middle Schoolers

For middle schoolers, delve deeper into aspects of consent's relevance beyond just physical safety. Build awareness of active, attentive listening skills and reciprocal agreements equalling healthier relationships. Educate them about dangers linked to blindly agreeing under pressures from peers; instead, stress strength drawn from within through autonomous thinking leads to healthier lives! Ensure continuous discussions highlight clear, enthusiastic verbal confirmation needed throughout lifelong relationships.

To High Schoolers

For high schoolers, let's cover all things related to consent in intimate connections. They should grasp understanding via verbal communication rather than relying solely on body language. Acknowledge distinctions between boundaries and pushing personal barriers; also encourage openness in finding what each person is comfortable with before taking any further steps and checking in along the way. Brief on how social media perpetuated idealisms may cloud accurate understandings of genuine consent; show the importance of questioning sociocultural norms! You must instill traits of respect, trust, and empathy when building long-lasting affectionate bonds!

DISCUSSING CONSENT IN DIFFERENT CONTEXTS

Talking to children concerning the concept of consent means helping them form wholesome views for their entire lifetime! Start age-appropriate conversations regarding consent in varying settings, ensuring a solid foundation of understanding respected by the next generation! Be there to offer comforting advice regarding all issues involving consent among pals, electronic chatter, romantic connections, or otherwise; these discussions could set the stage for stronger interpersonal growth later on, too!

Friendships

Teach children about consent reach—friendships are included in that category! Remind them to check boundaries before actions or games; additionally, ask prior to touching for permission because consent matters even outside intimacy types! Teach that everyone deserves room to say "no." Consistently chat with your kids about the importance of speaking up when something isn't okay. Reinforce a friendly environment where everyone feels safe and heard always.

Digital Interactions

In today's digital age, help raise responsible digital netizens! Strengthen kids' ability to knowingly safeguard private details and images shared digitally. Make them mindful before reposting, tagging, or interacting online. Discuss online footprint's potential impact on self and others in future scenarios so they learn to give genuine thought, teaching them to always seek permission before proceeding in the cybersphere, thus setting new standards for a healthier online culture!

Dating

As they enter their teen years, introduce meaningful chats about date-specific consent; equipping minds with the right tools means setting the groundwork for forming positive adult relationships. Emphasize open and honest conversation, mutual desires understood via "yes" instead of assuming compliance via silence or body language, and continuously check-in before making moves forward. Respect boundaries and communicate effectively throughout stages to preserve long-term relationship stability rooted in maturity.

Professional Settings

To develop an informed mindset in career pursuits, instruct youth regarding necessary skills for approaching work encounters properly! Explain the role of consensually interacting during meetings; clarify acceptable and unacceptable office actions like friendly touches. They should know physical boundaries extend far past obvious cases like handshakes into more ambiguous ones like fistbumps or side hugs; some people simply don't enjoy contact, so awareness levels are key. Help them see how gainfully using this info will build a pathway toward success in their future professional endeavors.

Medical and Health Situations

When kids encounter health matters, guide empathetic talks about body autonomy, especially highlighting their privilege in choosing what happens medically and involvement in decisions around the care journey ahead. Aid clarity by providing resources and activities that underscore self-advocating for trustworthy answers; allow your children to become self-assured through knowledge and experience openness during appointments, thereby shaping independent thinkers prepared to tackle future health challenges!

Personal Boundaries

Highlighting kids' understanding and communicating individual borders to themselves and others assists greatly in their quality of life! They hold exclusive rights to decide what makes them comfortable versus uncomfortable. By conveying preferences and honoring others' choices through mutual appreciation, both parties develop stronger, happier connections. Employing confidence in expressing feelings while accepting boundaries may vary for everyone else around us!

ADDRESSING THE ROLE OF POWER DYNAMICS IN RELATIONSHIPS

Have a chat with your kids on power dynamics found in everyday relations. It helps explain why some connections function easily while others encounter strife. We focus on identifying unequal control distribution so behaviors don't negatively affect happiness. Recognizing usual imbalances include pushing-pulling patterns, emotional distancing, fear-evoking, and shaming tactics, and offering solutions promoting reciprocal balancing! This results in more fulfilling human interactions by reducing negative impacts from misused powers! Grow closer through improved awareness nurtured by this exploration of power management.

The Demand-Withdrawal Dynamic

Have a conversation with your children regarding the classic situation where one party tends to pressure and coerce, whereas another tries to escape confrontations, commonly known as the "demand-withdrawal dynamic." Share experiences about how it leads to disputes or stalemates, emotional barriers, and discomfort. Suggest ways to foster effective interaction among each other through empathetic discussions focusing on resolvable solutions. Be a receptive listener as well as a vocal speaker, ensuring mutual understanding.

The Distancer-Pursuer Dynamic

Introduce yourselves and your kids to the distancer-pursuer pattern, where one party desires physical contact, companionship, or assistance, whereas another looks to become self-sufficient and distance themselves from similar caregiving gestures despite both wanting some level of mutual aid or help. Highlight possible difficulties arising due to this relationship structure, like suffocation and loneliness. Offer opportunities to appreciate each other's perspectives and brainstorm adaptive ideas as an answer to strengthening bonds based on both individual requirements and joint efforts!

The Fear-Shame Dynamic

Discuss the fear-ashamedness dynamic, which might obstruct people from freely articulating their desires, longings, or frailties because of previous incidents or social pressure. Illuminate how this dynamic could harm open and truthful chat, familiarity, and confidence in one another. Encourage setting up an atmosphere where there won't be any judging and giving shelter to the feeling of self-sympathy. Motivate embracing their partner in rising above dread and shyness through counseling when required.

Healthy Power Dynamics in Relationships

Give down-to-earth suggestions for establishing healthy power dynamics within relationships. Put emphasis on sharing respect, straightforward discussion, and reciprocal decisions. Urge fair allocation of power, stimulating problem-solving by working together and arriving at amicable settlements. Speak about conserving unique personalities and private restrictions through fortifying union and dependence. The recommended action plan includes sustained advancement and studying within the connection, propping up each other's desired goals and individual growth.

Recognizing and Addressing Imbalances

It's crucial to acknowledge and deal with imbalances in power dynamics within relationships. Encourage self-reflection and open conversations to disclose styles of management or dominance, disproportionate participation, or uneven treatment. Debate the function of agreement, boundaries, and tactful conversation in fixing anomalies. Advocate getting specialist guidance if essential to cope with intricate conditions or recover from earlier affliction.

Cultivating Empathy and Emotional Intelligence

Create harmony in relationships by inspiring and teaching regard and consciousness of each other's feelings and experiences. Appeal to really comprehending instead of criticizing or refuting another person's inner life experiences. Arouse emotive regulation knowledge to contemplate complications adequately. Bring awareness to the significance of acknowledging and addressing power imbalances based on gender, race, or other societal factors.

NAVIGATING DIFFICULT CONVERSATIONS ABOUT BOUNDARIES AND CONSENT

To keep children safe and build strong, trusting relationships, adults must talk with them about setting boundaries and gaining consent. These talks should convey warmth, respect, listening skills, and mutual appreciation—especially so younger folks can confidently share how they feel without fear of negative consequences or judgment from grownups.

Why It's Important to Respect Boundaries and Consent

Stress the significance of valuing boundaries and permission in sustaining strong connections and guaranteeing individual protection. Make clear that every person possesses the entitlement to govern what happens to their body and establish restrictions on close interaction and private areas. Elaborate on how regard for constraints and authorization generates an ambiance of confidence, esteem, and psychological wellness.

Exploring Personal Space

Talk about having their own personal space. Personal space means creating boundaries so they feel comfortable and secure. Examples include keeping some distance from others and wanting privacy. Reflect together on times when someone might cross into their personal spaces. How did it affect them? What could they do differently next time? Remember, taking care of the kids includes protecting their personal space!

Recognizing Unwanted Touch

Speak with your young ones regarding undesirable touch and aid them in appreciating their inner thoughts and sentiments related to them. Inquire about their experiences whenever someone touches them without approval. Promise them that no one ever has the right to put their hands on anyone else against their wishes— not even family members, acquaintances, friends, and so on. Assist them in discovering ways to say "no" if ever requested to be touched incorrectly. Remind them over and again: it's not their mistake; their emotions matter plenty, and that self-preservation always comes first.

Understanding Consent in Actions and Requests

Help your kids recognize that agreeing to things goes further than bodily closeness and comprises deeds, appeals, and undertakings. Educate them on cases wherein an individual wants them to execute something they don't fancy doing and how they can manage these kinds of conditions. Motivate them to concentrate on their particular necessities and suspicions and state "no" while feeling troubled or hesitant. Underscore the worthiness of being honest and following through on their gut feelings.

Reinforce Positive Affirmations

Finish your conversational exchange by confirming constructive declarations regarding their privileges, freedom, and limits. Advocate for them to believe in their instincts, converse on their behalf, and search out aid when required. Reassure them that you shall safeguard and sustain them.

PROMOTING COMMUNICATION AND NEGOTIATION SKILLS IN RELATIONSHIPS

Making sure efficient correspondence and settlement skills are established inside partnerships is indispensable for nurturing insightfulness, solving divergences, and fortifying robust bonds. By educating our youth on these imperative capabilities, we provide them with the capacity to negotiate human interactions with sympathy, regard, and the skill to come across commonplace remedies. This topic concentrates on instructing the next generation on effective methods to propel amicability, accord concurrence, and develop strong relationships. It introduces easygoing suggestions and techniques that aid youth in upholding associations, settling issues, and preserving nutritious and cooperative alliances. Teach them the tips below.

Be Observant

Advocate for your youngsters to remain mindful of their inner states and the actions of others so as to comprehend the workings of a connection better. Guide them to focus on non-verbal clues like body gestures and pitch since these could generate helpful glimpses into the yearnings and moods of other people.

Set the Communication Straight

Emphasize the significance of transparent and sincere interchange in relationships. Coax your children to verbalize themselves truthfully and cordially utilizing "I" statements to divulge their opinions and inclinations. Spur energetic concentration and acceptance of others' viewpoints to shape a sheltered arena for worthwhile debate.

You Can Compromise

Elucidate the idea of reconciliation and its position in sustaining healthy relationships. Educate your children that reconciliation signifies coming down midway wherever both sides feel listened to and their concerns resolved. Prompt them to stay agile and ready to make compromises, exhibiting that ties advance owing to concurrent awareness and versatility.

Never Compromise the Important Things

Assist your youngsters in realizing that although reconciliation is vital, some ideals or fundamental doctrines have to continue untouched. Direct them to distinguish their non-negotiables and to relate them firmly yet graciously. This provides them the capability to institute wholesome boundaries even though they pursue common interests.

Listen and Seek Clarification

Highlight the value of focused hearing and getting lucidity in conversation. Encourage your child to concentrate attentively on other individuals, asking questions to guarantee a full awareness of their standpoint. Urge them to restate and render back what they've heard, furthering a more profound bond and averting mistakes in judgment.

Have a Plan

Educate your children to tackle conversations by planning ahead. Stimulate them to pinpoint their purposes, fervent interests, and envisaged consequences ahead of indulging in dialogue. Such practice will permit them to present their wants successfully and collaborate for a favorable juncture for every party.

Have an Alternative Plan

Talk to your children about coming up with other ideas if the original idea doesn't work out. Brainstorm many choices since there usually are several solutions to any dilemma. Get creative and show them it might take trying new methods, which could eventually lead to the desired resolution after going through the process of trial and error. By doing so, you both enhance critical thinking skills while deepening bonds from shared experiences.

Be Stable

Coach your young ones to remain balanced during negotiations so that they don't lose focus and say things unintentionally. Calming down before responding helps one explain stuff more clearly; plus, listening attentively saves extra steps, thereby saving energy in resolving issues efficiently together. Assist them in managing tension via some activities listed here; regulating emotions strengthens relationships as we appreciate diverse viewpoints while finding constructive options collaboratively.

Be Calm

Teach little ones the virtues of speaking softly rather than shouting loudly whenever possible. Remind them that silence often communicates even louder messages yet respectfully by taking into account the partner's feelings before blurting out responses. In conflicts especially, pauses enable careful consideration instead of quick retaliation based on temporary emotions clouding judgment. Breathing deeply and counting before answering really works miraculously well in preserving great working conditions built upon trust earned through selfless acts of kindness. Sharing feelings constructively fosters closer connection due to increased understanding nurtured via those peaceful dialogues generated throughout this mutually beneficial activity.

Understand Your Goals and Theirs

Guide kids toward grasping their wants and another party's aspirations. This enables collaboration instead of constant competition. It gets everyone aligned via empathetic minds to find common ground through active participation. Whenever tasks demand completion collectively, success multiplies through teamwork resulting from this reciprocal approach honed over time to create lasting connections between folks sharing these cooperative values during negotiations.

Have the Right Mindset

Help them visualize favorable resolutions through constructive talks. The *can-do* optimism translating hopes into actions promotes win-win results, ensuring contentment is shared among participants once these productive conversations end. They should concentrate on gauging what will benefit most people involved rather than assuming everything boils down solely to individual victories or defeats. Building long-lasting associations happens when fruitful interactions occur regularly, thanks to open-mindedly tackling challenges as opportunities for joint progression. These encounters ultimately shape stronger partnerships via positive attitudes looking beyond disagreements toward successful problem-solving and a fair distribution of benefits felt by all engaged within this circle of influence.

Believe in Yourself

Empower kids to learn how to advocate appropriately for fulfillment amid differing opinions. Confidently articulating their position reaps tremendous benefits as courage instilled via earlier exposure carries forward later life applications. Trust develops into dependable self-assurance gained through positive reinforcement starting at home with loving parents setting examples emphasizing their capabilities. Overall, belief in their capacity strengthens coping mechanisms, enabling healthier interactions and empowering individuals ready to encounter assorted scenarios by adapting successfully because of support received during formative years.

Have an Open Mind to Suggestions

Train youngsters' ways of perceiving differing angles, opening up possibilities previously unnoticed. Exploring fresh ideas and considering contrasting opinions improves the chances of accomplishing set targets using combined knowledge. Respect displayed for various stances shows regard not only for one's own conclusions but also for hearing what others might contribute. Reaching agreements pleasing multiple sides emerges more feasibly through flexible thinking developed after examining additional choices available. Thus, keeping an open mind broadens horizons, leading toward greater overall success during and following successful exchanges involving different entities.

Don't Mix Personal Issues With Negotiation

Advise children to isolate current problems from previous matters or disputes already settled. Staying concentrated on the current issue prevents similar misunderstandings, magnifying hostility, and impeding satisfactory settlements. Avoiding irrelevant discussions frees mental blocks that can obstruct reasonable judgments and negatively influence future harmony. Resolvable differences handled amicably without dragging old grudges into unrelated arguments results in a clearer perspective that permits effective bargaining and culminates in equitable compromises respected by both parties. This allows a clearer atmosphere through honest conversation geared strictly toward addressing present questions versus letting lingering animosity distort perceptions.

Determine the Best Time for Discussion

Stress the significance of picking suitable moments to engage in communication and exchanging thoughts—ideally, when every party feels equally accessible in sharing respective insights unhindered. Appropriate timing ensures conducive settings that accommodate even the slightest negative mood swings and prevent them from stealing valuable concentration needed to reach the desired objectives. By picking the perfect moment for exchanging views wherein everyone genuinely desires to collaborate, the odds of a mutually successful outcome multiply. Leveraging optimal conditions propels efficient brainstorming sessions to end fruitfully because the initial preparation prevented impaired interaction from hindering productive problem-solving.

RECOGNIZING SIGNS OF UNHEALTHY RELATIONSHIPS AND ABUSE

Recognition skills are vital to grasp early warning signals indicating the development of unbalanced relationships that turn sour over time. When young minds absorb these tips, they are easily alerted when danger lurks ahead, preventing undesirable circumstances. Grownups must pass on know-how and teach young ones how to protect personal welfare whenever red flags surface. Learning steps to take whenever indicators show dysfunctional tendencies that could threaten the mental and physical equilibrium is really important.

Lack of Support

Highlight the need for wholesome support shared between intimate partnerships. Draw attention to deficiencies caused when unequal treatment surfaces or when requirements vital for prosperous interactions are neglected. Instead, teach them to offer adequate emotional, physical, and psychological upholding. Emphasize seeking out bondings endowed with compassionate caring devoid of selfish motivations standing opposed to positive relationship growth.

Envy or Jealousy

Train your children to identify feelings of envy or jealousy in their relationships. Envy and jealousy cause frequent mistrust; the urge to manage significant others' affairs; fear of losing a companionship; unease around pals, and more. Assure children that sound associations depend upon stability, admiration, and allowing companions exclusive autonomy.

Toxic Communication

Point out that hurtful and demeaning dialogue erodes trust and damages bonds within families and communities. Instruct your young ones to look for disrespectful language, including mockery and blaming attitudes, since even subtle jokes convey hidden sarcasm, causing resentment in people. Let them adopt gracious manners where they take pains to avoid such verbal attacks that undermine feelings of worthiness!

Resentment

Highlight common indicators of unforgiving conduct leading toward bitterness. These include recurring animosity between partners, harbored anger against one another, and unwillingness to talk about issues honestly or work toward equitable solutions as a team. Mention that overcoming problems requires direct yet loving confrontation. Rather than brooding in silence or bottled-up fury, communicate feelings respectively in peaceable ways. When done correctly, this leads couples closer emotionally after tackling troubles cooperatively rather than assuming negative beliefs!

Controlling Behaviors

Give your little ones tips on recognizing controlling behavior by pointing out telltale traits such as persistent micromanagement or wishing to influence every minor detail in the lives of loved ones. Emphasize their need to choose assertive habits while being receptive. This includes preserving an appropriate degree of independence in decision-making and resisting coercion while simultaneously accepting joint responsibilities.

Patterns of Disrespect

You should help your child appreciate dignified treatment within close relationships so their innate esteem remains stable through adulthood. It may begin with acknowledging certain rudiments like regular scornful glances, calling names, or constant condemnation because these things dampen the spirit and cultivate insecurity whenever a family doesn't offer courtesies sincerely.

Dishonesty

While helping your children learn healthy relationship qualities, stress the significance of truthfulness and straightforwardness since deceitfulness, secrecy, fabrications, or reneging obligations steadily corrode interpersonal security. Thus, make sure your children realize the need to form dependable ties founded upon openness and authenticity, enabling both parties to confide in each other without fear or doubts holding back, thus fostering wholesome bonds grounded on honesty and responsibility.

Constant Stress

You must instruct your young ones regarding the potential consequences of stress on relationships. Highlight that sustained apprehension, fright, or edginess when linked romantically may strain partnership ties since individuals don't experience calmness or serenity around the partner anymore—resulting in more distress. Direct them to pay heed by figuring out whether or not continuous worry persists throughout connection; then suggest finding emotional solace inside romantic associations—so peace ensues during future days together.

Negative Financial Behaviors

Educate your children about the role money plays in intimate connections to protect them from conceivably damaging factors later on. They must comprehend how attempts at controlling, dominating funds, or squandering assets might weaken their association bond unless the two collaborate with each other to take ownership of their collectively managed possessions plus fiscal planning by discussing matters freely.

Lost Relationships

Explain to your kids how unwholesome attachment dynamics tend to push apart families and friends over time; this happens when one member feels forced to cater to others, leading to gradual isolation and detachment from cherished allies since they seem too occupied with meeting needs of another person instead of nurturing treasured affiliations.

Ignoring Your Needs

Instruct your children to spot if their requirements get repeatedly rejected or overlooked while being part of a loving relationship. Teach them to have self-respect and take the initiative to assert honest wants. Doing so forms solid bonds centered around understanding and respect since individuals who grasp their own rights will instinctually favor mates who view them as equals with parallel wants and desires that warrant consideration, too. Therefore, showcase advantages derived from standing up for themselves in love affairs.

Walking on Eggshells

Train your kids on how skittishly navigating a sweetheart's feelings and reactions harms your kinship since it cultivates a climate of unease by never truly sensing secure or safe around them owing to frequent upsets or explosiveness—such conditions lead to a possibly volatile and maybe even hazardous connection should the alarm be raised over potential mistreatment or damage caused through these types of interactions. Remind little ones to always think about shielding their physical and emotional welfare by choosing secure relationships built on trust and reciprocity so that life is enjoyable and anxiety-free.

Hoping for Change

Help younglings detect repeating scenarios when they keep wishfully expecting modifications in their partner's traits without observing actual advancement. Show them this typically stems from insufficient determination, exertion, or obligation from the person they want to alter toward them, thus impeding satisfactory modification from occurring in close proximity between them. Encourage your child to focus on joy and contentment individually whenever necessary changes fail to occur within current interpersonal connections.

Lack of Self-Care

Guide your junior to comprehend the significance of looking after themselves and gratifying personal aspirations irrespective of whether they clash or agree with someone else's interests. Stress that repeatedly sacrificing individual wants just to please or go along with others could mean existing in an unwholesome association. Instill in them that taking care of themselves first and knowing that they, too, have rights and deserve joy is vital for both sides to function successfully together.

PROMOTING RESPECT AND EQUALITY IN ALL RELATIONSHIPS

Children must realize how crucial respecting others is no matter what. We want kids to grasp interdependence and similarity in humanity since the world already has enough differences between people based on caste systems or hierarchical biases. So if young minds grow up having sympathy and genuine regard toward diverse cultures by learning to relate and comprehend one another via thoughtful words rather than impulse actions, then discord reduces, allowing space for constructive growth where unity can flourish. Hence, encouraging education on respecting diversity and reciprocal affirmation ensures mutually beneficial living conditions throughout entire communities.

Understanding Respect

Show your little ones about admiring others, especially those dissimilar to them. Kids need to understand that every person is unique. They might vary physically, intellectually, socially, or psychologically, but nevertheless, everyone deserves equal attention and fair judgment free of negative assumptions rooted in stereotypes or hearsay opinions instead of actual proof. That way, we help kids discover their moral compass earlier, enabling them to live decently alongside varied groups once grown-ups without feeling the urge to belittle or hurt those less advantaged by birthright due to lack of familiarity or inexperience interacting.

Promoting Open Communication

Make sure your children grasp why forthright discussion matters when maintaining dignified cooperation between contrasting social categories. Educated individuals will be conscious of their behaviors and attitudes impacting society plus would preferably engage in reasonable conversations void of prejudices learned from elders. Therefore, raise your voice against discriminatory slurs and promote productive chats focused on reaching a common ground while accepting people's varying situations arising from misfortune or choice since nobody controls everything destined.

Embracing Differences

Help children perceive differences as something valuable instead of regarding them negatively so that they may form friendships among varied kinds of people. It benefits everyone involved directly or indirectly, provided by exposure to variety. Celebrate diversity as something natural and noteworthy, like colorful flowers blooming together, because our environment affects us collectively despite individual differences, making human relations richer.

Challenging Stereotypes and Bias

Provide children insights into harmful labels and beliefs continuously generating unfair treatment among peers or colleagues. Discuss how these preformed judgments could cause exclusion or underestimation, leading to more serious problems like bullying, which are avoidable with mindful thoughts. Guide kids into examining these commonly accepted myths ingrained inside their subconscious by conditioning so that they analyze the logic behind certain expectations, hence reframing any potential detrimental behavior in school or workplaces.

Promoting Empathy and Empowering Others

Help your young ones develop sympathy toward others and how they view things. Guide them to show warmth and back those facing difficulties or unfairness. Give your children the power to stick up for anyone who might receive unfriendliness because of who they are.

Addressing Conflict Constructively

Train your kids on dealing with arguments properly. Nudge them to share their thoughts directly yet considerately and pay attention when others reply. Educate them on negotiation techniques so both sides end contentedly.

BYSTANDER INTERVENTION

We should encourage kids to stand up for others even if it doesn't impact them personally—bystander interventions. The message to get across is recognizing and stopping harm when seen. When it comes to giving approval, teach ways to say yes or no honestly, plus methods that will help make certain neither party feels coerced. Raising awareness on these topics could lead to stronger communities and lower levels of hurt caused by violations or manipulation (which happen regardless of age).

Disrupt the Situation

Instruct your kids to step in when something seems off between two individuals. Suggest making noise and grabbing extra sets of eyes nearby or saying, "Hey, what's going on here?" to interrupt any foul play. Point out that acting fast means potentially reducing issues later and showing everyone else that mistreatment won't slide! These steps assist in diffusing and sending a clear "no" toward wrong actions. Share useful tricks to stop awkwardness before it escalates or hurts someone further. Work together to create kinder spaces today.

Confront the Harasser

Show your children good approaches to tackle people causing unwanted troublesome circumstances... and some pointers on how. Focus on maintaining poise, posture, and vocal pitch. Make sure your little ones know this does not mean losing manners or coming across as rude. Urge them to call out harmful acts since standing up for others often helps shut down hurtful actions or unethical norms. Remember to remind your mini humans that being bold doesn't always need huge courage either; straightforward but firm dialogue can work wonders, too!

Don't Act Alone

Learn along with your young ones that group efforts during difficult scenarios actually improve success. Stress-gathering backup reinforces their stance and intimidates those aiming to cause trouble. Overall, show them the benefits of teamwork versus handling upsets solo. With your combined effort (plus maybe a few more friendly faces), you might gain more positive outcomes vs. attempting resolution alone.

Understand Your Privilege and Speak Up

Educate yourself and your little ones by clarifying the advantages they have and why it makes them capable champions fighting against misbehavior and unfair treatment. Cover how having special opportunities grants more voice strength and possibly higher accept-ability, challenging improper habits. Motivate them to utilize assets gifted through fortune or birthplace for the greater good and defend struggling peers without the same level of influence yet.

Set Expectations and Step In

When teaching your kids important values, establish strong guidelines. Promote voicing opposition and physically helping if others face harmful behaviors or are forced into uncomfortable situations. Everyone deserves equal comfort; therefore, they should take initiative when possible (even if only by lending verbal support). Together, set a benchmark wherein watching out for each other becomes standard.

Take Action Online

Assist your kiddos in understanding that, similar to real-life cases involving others facing hardships or offenses, stepping up online is imperative, as well as doing the right thing. The more voices that stand tall together against harmful content and behaviors... the faster positive changes occur within a safer virtual reality. By modeling responsible citizenship at early ages and encouraging online allies, your little ones grow valuable skills ready to lead society's evolution toward a brighter web world everyone enjoys exploring!

Focus on the Needs of the Target

Educate your children on the significance of listening to and caring for individuals affected by unwanted conduct. Making certain they grasp this includes acknowledging emotional pains and showing empathetic responses. Reinforce offering backing, too. Most importantly, ensuring understanding lies in validating the personal choices of these mistreated people whose feelings and free will deserve recognition and respect under all circumstances. Such lessons plant seeds of humanity and selflessness, preparing the next generation to promote improved societies built on compassionate foundations.

Be Proactive

Cultivate a sense of responsibility in your little ones to monitor events for anyone needing aid because no one else stepped forward yet. Help them recognize clues predicting troublesome conditions and empower gut feelings and when signaling help is necessary. They must act decisively and not wait like passive viewers but rather turn into active change agents safeguarding fellow humans. Shaping their character now creates confident problem solvers determined to shape healthier communities over time.

Support the Target

Show your young ones ways to come to other's aid when dealing with undesirable behavior. Offer practical solutions to bring comfort and guidance to restore confidence during unsettling moments. Share options allowing victims paths to professional counselors and accessible reporting sources ready to listen actively. You and your growing kids will become better equipped to respond promptly on behalf of those unfairly treated due to this knowledge foundation now ingrained.

Bystander involvement, along with authorization lifestyles, would be the main elements meant for growing safe locations exactly where esteem really does prevail. By simply educating kids about bystander treatment and even developing the tradition centered on authorization, you enable them to function as important contributors in producing optimistic modifications. Simply by deteriorating scenarios, dealing with offenders, operating jointly, figuring out expertise, and anticipating the environment, not to mention performing things online, your young ones can play a role in designing an additional admiring and accommodating culture. Help them focus on their goals instead of their impulses, help them be productive, and support those affected by distractions. Let's work together to create new traditions where we can all look out for each other and make sure everyone feels safe and welcome.

7

SEXUAL HEALTH AND REPRODUCTION

Discussions related to sex and reproduction are integral parts of humankind's living; hence, it's necessary to educate our kids with precise info, generate beneficial perspectives, and permit them to determine by themselves. By adopting an affirmative perspective together with thoughtful dialogues that emphasize safety and ease in getting knowledge about this natural component of everyday life, we will manage to set up environments that allow our children to question freely and explore this natural part of life.

The conversation associated with sexual health and reproduction is a challenging job; however, it's required to provide our juniors with appropriate info and directions. Here are different approaches meant to aid you at the start of talks, form a tranquil atmosphere, and guarantee a constructive attitude when presenting subjects linked to sex. We will investigate methods for promptly kickstarting the conversations along with making a cozy space so your kids will feel calm while inquiring about things or disclosing their sentiments.

By dispelling wrong beliefs, misconceptions, and prejudices, our aim here is to get a better grasp alongside admiration of the human lifecycle's complexity once we learn all of this correctly. When kids reach maturity, it is crucial that you teach them different techniques to avoid unwanted pregnancies and sexually transmitted infections (STIs) via the employment of prophylactic devices like condoms and oral birth control tablets. It is important to study varied alternatives before opting for any means and stress the value of responsibly made decisions regarding healthcare, emotional balance, and overall contentment connected to choosing contraception methods.

BASICS OF SEXUAL HEALTH AND HYGIENE

Grasping fundamentals regarding sexual health and hygiene is crucial. Coaching your teenagers on these themes allows them to build wholesome customs and deal with their own bodies effectively. This topic concentrates on giving reliable, encouraging tips with regard to standard sexual health and hygiene, featuring the significance of proper care, interaction, and timely action.

Cleaning Private Areas

Ensure your children know that keeping a correct degree of tidiness in private areas is critical and also stress the significance of regularly cleaning those regions with delicate cleansing products like mild soaps mixed with gentle hot water. Prompt them to check the areas where skin may bunch since moisture can cause unease along with microbe infections if it is not attended to properly.

Changing Condoms

Speak to your children about the benefits of using condoms as contraceptives, along with defending against contagious diseases connected to sexual intercourse. Instruct them condoms must be put into use accurately and disposed of after use. They are not to be reused. Bring attention to the advantages of utilizing brand-spanking new prophylactics in order to keep guard against STIs plus unwanted fertility.

Emptying the Bladder After Sex

Talking about the importance of emptying the bladder after sexual activity is crucial since such action assists in flushing away any type of microbes that might have gone into the urethra, lessening the danger associated with urinary tract infections. Motivate them to get accustomed to emptying their own bladder immediately following intimate interludes.

Washing Before and After Sex

Inform your children about the significance of cleansing previous to and also right after sexual intercourse. Talk through the particular merits of exercising sound cleaning habits to avoid germs and unpleasant smells. Encourage them to speak to their partners about individual health care and hygiene and to make sure mutual neatness allows for a comfortable and fun practical experience.

Douching Is Not Recommended

Make known to your kids that douching isn't recommended due to the fact the vaginal area possesses the ability to purify itself. It contains an appropriate ecological equilibrium involving healthy germs supporting it to stay wholesome. Inform your children that douching could mess up this specific stability, leading to a greater chance of infections.

Not Ignoring Unusual Signs

Stress the relevance of focusing on their bodies and paying attention to any sort of odd warning signs regardless of how insignificant they may seem. Educate them to pay attention to any kind of modifications, unease, itching, discharge, or anything else unusual that may showcase the possible infection or even another health issue. Remind them to seek health assistance whenever they possess virtually any worries.

Cleaning Sex Toys

If your teenagers are using sex toys, share the need for cleansing them effectively. Make clear that these kinds of tools need to be scrubbed using warm water and gentle soap both before and after each use. Recommend purchasing device-secure cleanup items to take care of sanitation and maintain proper hygiene.

Seeking Professional Guidance

Instruct your kids to look for specialized direction anytime it relates to their sexual well-being as well as their health. Direct them to health treatment experts similar to physicians or maybe sexual health centers for correct tips, suggestions, and examinations. Educate them on why selecting an established healthcare supplier will allow them to respond to any problems as well as queries they will experience.

DISCUSSING SEXUALLY TRANSMITTED INFECTIONS AND PREVENTION

Beginning conversations relating to germs transferred via sexual acts is essential when trying to improve sexual welfare while encouraging reliable conduct. With constructive and relaxing help and advice, you can encourage your teenagers to make sensible sexual decisions to avoid catching any STIs. The main objective here is to offer instructional and positive chats around STIs and prevention, emphasizing the importance of education, communication, and practicing safe behaviors.

Understanding STIs

Inform them STIs are spread by way of sexual contact, like oral, anal, or vaginal sex. Highlight that it is essential to learn about the different kinds of STIs and their signs. Make sure to highlight how critical it is to learn what the likely consequences could be.

Promoting Education

Teach your kids the importance of being knowledgeable about STIs to stop the spread of them. Communicate the distinct categories of STIs—such as chlamydia, gonorrhea, human papillomavirus (HPV), and cold sores (herpes), together with HIV or AIDS. Provide accurate and age-appropriate information. Detailed knowledge of every single illness should include its distribution methods, indications, screenings, and accessible medical care treatment options.

Practicing Safe Behaviors

Have a talk with your children about the importance of practicing safe behaviors to prevent the transmission of STIs. Guide them in terms of applying defense approaches, for example, condoms, while engaging in sex play. In particular, concentrate on the frequent and proper usage of condoms. Also, focus attention on two different alternatives obtainable: one designed for guys and another with respect to women.

Getting Tested Regularly

Encourage regular STI testing as a protective level intended for overall sexual and physical condition. Make clear that STI exams will need to be conducted even without indicators present, especially after new sexual encounters. Encourage your teenagers to understand the importance of getting tested, the testing process, and the availability of confidential and supportive healthcare services.

Promoting Vaccination

Speak to your teenagers regarding the opportunity of receiving vaccines to prevent certain STIs, such as the HPV vaccination to help prevent cervix cancer tumors, amongst other cancers, besides the hepatitis B vaccine shielding opposite hepatitis B virus (HBV) transferal. Ask them to seek counseling from qualified personnel pertaining to the safety measures and accessibility of distinct vaccines.

Dispelling Myths and Reducing Stigma

Talk about common myths and misconceptions around STIs and share with your kids how easy it is to end up with an STI, despite one's culture or perhaps lifestyle. Focus on minimizing the stigmatization connected to STIs in addition to addressing others using under-standing, regard, and assistance.

EXPLAINING CONTRACEPTION METHODS AND THEIR EFFECTIVENESS

Be certain your teenage kids fully grasp diverse contra-ception methods, including the different levels of protection they offer to help them select a safer sex life-style and make informed decisions and conclusions. Providing comforting, trustworthy advice assists them to feel confident and ready to handle those choices. We must concentrate on conveying correct information and urging them to establish private judgments that meet particular necessities. The goal here is to educate about a variety of birth controls and their potency so your teenage kids possess a good understanding of their options and get equipped for safe intercourse.

Importance of Contraception

It's necessary to talk about using contraceptives to stop unwanted pregnancies and improve sexual welfare. Outline how this permits your kids to decide whether or not they wish to begin a family and to decide when they wish to do so. Being able to prevent pregnancy grants young people the power to attain educational background goals, professional ambitions, plus other desired objectives beforehand while still enjoying a healthy sex life.

Hormonal Methods

There are many types of hormonal methods of contraception, including oral contraceptive pills, implant treatments, injections, and uterine bands. They can prevent unwanted pregnancy by reducing the chances of fertilization. Offer clarification on precisely how hormone methods work either through preventing sperm from accessing the womb or by adjusting ovulation. Make sure they know that hormonal methods do not protect against STIs and require a prescription from a healthcare professional.

Long-Acting Reversible Contraception

Educate children concerning long-acting reversible contraception processes such as intrauterine devices (IUDs) and contraceptive implants. These offer long-lasting security against unwanted pregnancy and do not require consistently remembering to take a pill or have a condom to hand. They will need to have a consultation with the medical staff pertaining to the right placement along with elimination.

Fertility Awareness-Based Methods

Educate your kids about fertility awareness-based methods (FABMs), additionally referred to as normal family planning, which requires checking monthly menstrual routines in addition to figuring out fertile as well as sterile time spans. Detail the reliability of FABMs whenever utilized accurately as well as persistently. They will need to know to keep detailed track of cycles and body functions.

Emergency Contraception

It's important for individuals to know about emergency contraception—also referred to as the morning-after pill—and what it does. Emergency contraception is used right after unprotected sex in case of a contraceptive failure. It must be accepted as soon as possible for the best results!

Sterilization

Talk over permanent methods of contraception like tube closure just for females as well as vasectomy for males. Explain that sterilization really is the ultimate determination and must be looked into cautiously due to the fact it isn't always irreversible.

Effectiveness and Factors Influencing Effectiveness

Offer a summary of the effectiveness rates for different contraception methods, focusing on the way effectiveness may differ based on correct usage, dependency, and individual factors. Make sure they know about consumer mistake, medication interactions, as well as preexisting medical circumstances that might influence the results of these different contraceptive methods.

Individualized Decision-Making

Highlight the significance of individualized decision-making once choosing any contraceptive method. Motivate individuals to look into unique preferences, lifestyles, overall health elements, as well as long-term reproduction targets when picking out a strategy that fits their desires in addition to beliefs.

ADDRESSING QUESTIONS ABOUT PREGNANCY AND CHILDBIRTH

Pregnancy, as well as childbirth, is a natural part of life. You will find your children will have questions and concerns about these things. We can aid our children through this kind of lifetime-altering experience by supporting and comforting them and guiding them to maneuver through this kind of journey with assurance and knowledge. Providing your teenage kids with facts about pregnancy and childbirth and also motivating trustworthy info sources assists them in embracing this specific voyage utilizing a hopeful frame of mind.

Understanding Pregnancy

Explain the basics of pregnancy. Explain how fertilization happens and move on to discuss the growth of a developing baby in the womb. Explore the typical bodily transformations as well as emotional shifts women go through throughout pregnancy. Emphasize that all of these modifications are standard and the importance of self-care.

Confirming Pregnancy

Address common questions about confirming pregnancy, discuss problems such as when to take a pregnancy test and how to determine its reliability, along with talking to health practitioners. Concentrate on getting started with early prenatal attention, along with setting up communication with a medical doctor.

Prenatal Care

Shine a light on the value of prenatal care in maintaining a healthy pregnancy. Concentrate on just how frequent check-ups, screenings, and tests may help monitor the mom's as well as the infant's well-being. Promote your kids to take part in their parental care simply by consulting concerns in addition to conversing worries together with their healthcare provider.

Healthy Lifestyle During Pregnancy

Engage your younglings in a chat concerning the value of keeping up a wholesome lifestyle while pregnant. Focus on matters involving diet regime, exercise routine, weight increase, and detrimental elements that might endanger the unborn baby. Highlight the importance of looking after themselves, controlling worry, and obtaining ample rest in preserving a healthy gestation.

Common Discomforts and Concerns

Speak to your young kids about typical problems and worries that women usually deal with during pregnancy. Chat about subjects like nausea, tiredness, back soreness, and mental modifications, emphasizing that all these issues are generally experienced but aren't necessarily serious concerns. Advise your daughters to consult medical care professionals for recommendations for easing any uneasiness that they could be experiencing.

Labor and Delivery

Provide information about the occurrence of labor and giving birth to your kids. Go over various aspects of labor like the different levels and the alternatives for managing pain, the contribution of health professionals at the time, and the essence of having maternity schemes to assist parents in making knowledgeable choices appropriate to them and keep protected. Emphasize that each birth circumstance varies so that individuals must not compare experiences and take into account their decisions according to their specific conditions and requirements.

Postpartum Period

Talk to your young ones about what occurs following the birthing procedure. Talk about topics relating to postpartum healing, getting accustomed emotionally as well as caring for the infant, highlighting the significance of taking care of oneself and searching for aid from the nearest and dearest, and building a connection with the newborn. Recommend talking to health specialists for advice related to following up on caring for moms right after childbirth as well as sorting out any troubles encountered.

Breastfeeding and Infant Nutrition

Talk about nursing babies naturally and advantageously with your kids. Talk over recurring questions in relation to nursing methods, positioning, and dealing with issues that come up. Bring up the accessibility of assistance and learning materials to guarantee a gratifying breastfeeding experience. Appreciate that everyone possesses the authority to select the feeding technique that suits them and their baby.

Emotional Well-Being

Make sure to focus on the significance of being emotionally content during gestation and giving birth among your young ones. Speak about how it's ordinary to sense mixed feelings like happiness and enthusiasm in addition to panic and apprehension. Advocate transparency with close friends and family members, doctors, or psychological well-being professionals for backing and direction all through the emotive expedition.

PROMOTING THE IMPORTANCE OF REGULAR CHECK-UPS AND HEALTHCARE

Ensure you teach your children how essential routine checkups are, together with quality care. These appointments are useful for tracking general health and dealing with any likely difficulties. By fostering the significance of repeated examinations along with adequate treatment, we encourage our children to manage their own health and look after themselves. Make sure you stress the importance of regular checkups and that they know that anything disclosed is confidential between them and the healthcare provider.

Preventive Care

To begin with, make certain you educate your young ones concerning the significance associated with preventive maintenance regarding overall health. Clarify which consistent visits will let health experts execute inspections, track down important signals, and determine basic health standing. Place emphasis on the fact that preventive attention facilitates uncovering prospective complications quickly and also increases the odds involving therapeutically profitable cures, which lessens their particular influence regarding the overall healthy state.

Establishing a Relationship With a Healthcare Provider

Make sure your kids build links with dependable health-related service providers. Remark on the merits associated with owning any principal health practitioner or maybe some other healthcare staff who's aware of their particular health background and then gives adapted therapy as well as guide them about avoidance measures, not to mention overall health progress.

Frequency of Check-ups

Chat with your daughters and sons regarding appropriate appointments depending on age, sex, and specific health requirements. Place emphasis on the fact that periodic evaluations could differ according to each individual's scenario. Recommend going to a general practitioner at least yearly for an all-inclusive evaluation of overall health.

Comprehensive Physical Examinations

Converse with your children about the usefulness of extensive bodily inspections amid consultations. Mention how medical care specialists measure vitally significant indicators, undertake tangible checks, and demand blood work exams to evaluate varied aspects of overall health. Signify the function of these analyses in finding prospective afflictions and pinpointing matters requiring adjustment.

Preventive Screenings

Speak about the significance of preventive screenings as part of regular check-ups. Highlight widespread tests like hypertension dimension, cholesterol evaluations, most cancer screenings, plus vaccinations. Emphasize that preventive screenings can help recognize health conditions before warning signs occur. Early recognition lets you get better remedies, which often lead to more desirable final results.

Health Education and Counseling

Mention the significance associated with frequent checkups and giving essential information when seeing your health practitioner. Healthcare specialists can provide guidance regarding balanced lifestyle conclusions, disease prevention, and management of chronic conditions. Encourage your kids to take advantage of this valuable information to make informed decisions about their health.

Mental Health Support

Talk about the value of addressing mental health during check-ups. Mention how the healthcare practitioners may provide assistance, offer screening, and make recommendations for psychological health issues. Point out that mental conditions need to be taken care of just as seriously as bodily conditions and people must understand there are no stigmas connected with acquiring aid when struggling with mental health troubles.

Proactive Approach to Self-Care

Encourage your young ones to adopt a proactive approach to self-care beyond check-ups. Express the magnitude of retaining a healthy way of living, for example, exercises, diet program supervision, satisfactory relaxation, stress management, as well as steering clear of dangerous routines. Concentrate on which specific actions and behaviors greatly impact total health.

PROVIDING ACCURATE INFORMATION ABOUT ABORTION AND ADOPTION

Unfortunately, unplanned pregnancies do occur. It is good to have a conversation with your children about precise information about available alternatives, for example, abortion and adoption. Ensure that you offer beneficial and tranquilizing counsel to your kids so that they have easy access to applicable resources to assist them in picking selections consistent with their particular scenarios. You should aim to give exact information pertaining to abortion and adoption in a non-judgemental manner, emphasizing the importance of choice, access to resources, and compassionate support.

Understanding Abortion

Explain that abortion sometimes involves an operation that terminates a pregnancy. Signify that you will find distinct approaches toward performing abortion procedures; one may utilize tablets and another in clinic operations. Focus on supplying current and correct information associated with basic safety, legitimacy, and availability of abortion services in your region.

Accessing Abortion Services

Briefly explain why having access to secure as well as legalized abortions is required if an individual wants to terminate a pregnancy. Talk over how to recognize reputable professionals, facilities, or even organizations that offer confidential and supportive services. Direct attention toward the specific time period for consultations in addition to knowledge of any sort of legal specifications.

Emotional Support and Counseling

Abortion can be a very emotional time for people. Remind them that seeking out emotional help and therapy sessions would help individuals make their decision. Encourage individuals to connect with trusted healthcare providers, counselors, or support organizations that offer non-judgmental support and guidance.

Understanding Adoption

For those who don't want or cannot raise a kid but desire to ensure they get into a caring environment, adoption can certainly function as an alternative solution. Talk about variances between available forms of adoption like open adoption (where birth parents and adoptive parents maintain some level of contact) and closed adoption (where no contact is maintained).

Adoption Process and Resources

Acknowledge the requirement to present knowledge regarding adoption processes, such as the lawful measures required, house study, and pairing with foster parents. Inform individuals concerning reliable companies that could direct these through the method and provide support and resources. Emphasize the importance of considering the long-term implications and making an informed decision about adoption.

Emotional Support for Adoption

Speak to them regarding the emotive elements involving planning an adoption. Understand it will require great courage for many people to decide on setting up their own children to get adopted. Highlight the value of connecting with help groups who may lend emotional encouragement while creating significant conclusions like embracing an adoption procedure.

Making an Informed Decision

Spotlight the importance of making an informed decision that aligns with personal values, circumstances, and future goals. Remind your children that everyone's instance is specific; thus, there is no solitary remedy that suits almost everything. Inspire your kids to shell out occasions acquiring the right details, hunting assistance, and pondering the most obtainable solutions ahead of coming to a conclusion.

Non-Judgmental Approach and Compassionate Support

Underline the need for a warm and caring manner when referring to abortion along with adoption treatments. People sometimes require assistance in making decisions that harmonize with their particular worths as well as situations. Motivate sympathy, comprehending, and even regard intended for personal freedom and options associated with individuals undertaking those processes.

Ensuring Access to Comprehensive Reproductive Healthcare

Recommend the importance of comprehensive reproductive healthcare services that provide accurate information about all options, including abortion and adoption. Highlight the relevance involving assuring accessibility to secure and lawful abortion alternatives, adoption methods, and emotional sustainment. Advocate for regular attempts toward removing obstacles in addition to promoting the actual welfare and reproductive legal rights of all individuals.

Sharing appropriate tips regarding abortion and adoption should certainly always be considered critical if offering assistance to women facing unforeseen pregnancies. Supplying empathetic and non-judgmental suggestions may help your kids draw conclusions determined by their special instances, qualities, and potential desired goals. Using correct advice, connection to methods together with providers, psychological aid, and even mindset could assure them obtain the understanding and encouragement needed to address this kind of intricate possibility confidently, as well as having regard for everyone else.

8

FACING CHALLENGES AND HANDLING TOUGH QUESTIONS

Having conversations on topics surrounding intimacy could possibly be problematic under some circumstances, particularly if there are tricky queries coming from children. Even so, whenever all of us tackle these types of subject areas using serenity, knowing, with exact data, we can establish an environment within which our children feel risk-free in getting responses and figuring out their particular curiosity for awareness. This chapter works as a guide to commonly asked questions by kids about sex, offering strategies to handle these inquiries with confidence and grace.

Discover ways to react to questions from children with integrity and sincerity. Don't deliver deceptive or inaccurate information, mainly because it will cause perplexity and then misconception. In case anyone isn't unsure about the solution, be truthful about this and offer to find the information together, or maybe seek advice from a trusted source. Sex talks may include private principles and faiths. Encourage your children to provide feedback and look at differing points of view noncritically. Focus on how every person possesses different outlooks, which should be shown regard even though you are offering exact knowledge.

Talking over sexual subject matters could very well make grown-ups feel awkward but you should let your young ones know queries are welcome and answer honestly. Sharing that you're devoted to providing reliable facts might reduce feelings of unease or apprehension. Adult behavior may also help decrease anxiety by appearing calm while discussing the issue. Understand that not having solutions to their questions is okay. Encourage the younger generation to research details as a continuing project if you don't have the answers they seek. Assure them it's perfectly normal to declare "I am not sure" and then you can work jointly in solving things together. Developing interest along with an eagerness to discover combined encourages a stronger relationship between you both during future dealings.

Realize there might occur certain issues whereby youngsters need to communicate with medical practitioners or teachers who focus on specific subjects. Help youthful generations seek advice from authoritative references like general physicians, faculty guidance consultants, or learning materials suited for their age level. Make known skilled professionals manage accurate intelligence and resolve questions asked.

PREPARING FOR CHALLENGING AND UNCOMFORTABLE CONVERSATIONS

Having conversations about sex can get unsettling for several moms and dads or guardians. Still, being ready and keeping a favorable perspective after employing advantageous approaches allows us to tackle these topics with self-confidence and provide correct data that supports our young. The concentration here is to direct you to plan for hard and distressing conversations about sex through fostering instruction and developing a good mental state and backdrop.

Prepare for These Difficult Conversations

Be aware that communicating about sex may feel difficult or distressing. Realize the value of getting prepared in one's emotional and intellectual capacity when engaging in these types of exchanges. Bear in mind that being a care provider or guardian means delivering legitimate info as well as valuable tips and aids to assist in your children's physical growth advancement.

Educating Yourself

Make enough hours available for studying information pertaining to sex education and connected domains, including human body structure and functionality, procreation, well-being, protection and authorization, and others. Draw upon reliable assets like reading material, reports, and internet sites, or request expert counsel from proficient specialists within sex training to guarantee accuracy in the content given and appropriateness based on your little ones' age range.

Maintaining a Positive Attitude

Talk about this subject matter while retaining a positive attitude. Spotlight the significance of opening up talks and build an inviting atmosphere wherein your descendants tend to ask queries comfortably. Prepare yourself to hear unbiased and calm their anxieties by telling them that their passion is normal and wholesome. Having a constructive mind frame will certainly encourage reliance and make talking easier.

Keep This Difficult Conversation Short and Simple

Conversations relating to sex do not have to be prolonged, restorative, or intense. Breaking down details into simpler parts is often better understood by your juniors. Ensure clarifications meet their present stage of maturity and express using clear terms that are simple and sufficient for them to grasp. Center attention on handling individual questions sought after together with worry and apprehensions they possess.

Choose the Right Time and Place

Assess moments and conditions for the right time for these kinds of chats. Select peaceful and comfortable spots where both of you can stay undisturbed and tension-free. Arrange sessions during stress-free intervals so neither one of you is in haste. Producing a risk-less and comfy environment encourages frank conversations.

Using Everyday Opportunities

Seek out possible times throughout daily life to talk over subjects regarding sex normally. Draw upon televised series, movies, bulletins, or chats involving connections to bring up conversations. Such circumstances will render the issue appear more applicable and much less petrifying. Being vigilant plus observant of your junior's signals and fascination contributes greatly.

Be Prepared to Answer Tough Questions

Expect that youngsters might seek out complex plus unknown inquiries through a duration of sessions similar to this. Acquire the ability to handle issues correctly and suitably adapted for their years. If you do not have an answer to one of their questions, confess that truth and pledge to track down the answers for them. Motivate a spirit of interest plus desire to study, which maintains ongoing dialogue.

Addressing Personal Values and Beliefs

Realize that discussion associated with sexual matters typically intertwines private ideals and thinking. Make sure you address your own convictions and perceptions in a polite way. Prompt kids to reveal their individual opinions and insights, thus leading to being adaptable and tolerant of various ways of seeing things.

Providing Reassurance and Support

Console kids that you're reachable to settle inquiries or doubts whenever required. Make it known that dealing with sex-connected subjects happens while they grow older, and you shall aid and direct them when they need you. Give resource-filled items like books, webpages, or proper learning material tailored suitable for particular ages to deliver further details.

Celebrating Open Communication

Recognize that conveying subject matter related to sex between you two constitutes a key element of a bond between yourselves. Discussion on this subject matter demonstrates assurance, fondness, and promise toward their good health. With this backdrop to your relationship, you set up your child for making choices that are correct as well as instructed properly.

HANDLING QUESTIONS ABOUT PORNOGRAPHY AND EXPLICIT CONTENT

Living in the current digitally dependent world, kids could confront sexually graphic material and come to you with questions. It requires parental or guardians' attention to deal with subject areas associated with pornography using tranquility and awareness, along with exact information. Aiding and directing kids using supportive and confident advice can help them traverse complicated subjects while strengthening their sound comprehension of sexuality.

Define Pornography

Openly talk about this subject by characterizing exactly what porno indicates in applicable terminology pertaining to little ones. Clarify that pornography contains erotic supplies in the form of video, images, or text messages designed to inspire sensual emotions. Utilize languages suitable for a boy or girl's age along with apprehending potential.

Don't Let Porn Become a Taboo Subject

Support chatting on themes related to adult entertainment and underscore boys or girls being capable of turning to you should they possess queries on the topics. Do not let porn become a taboo subject or something they feel uncomfortable discussing with you, as it will result in them going elsewhere for information that may be unreliable. By sustaining an unbiased ambiance and passing on factual data, resolve their queries along with offering the right information.

Laughter Can Help

Utilize humor when deemed appropriate during subject matters entailing delicate issues. Chuckling might assist in alleviating pressure and also generate a more soothing environment. Even so, confirm that the chat remains polite plus doesn't subvert the weightiness connected with the question being debated.

Try Not to Overreact

Be mindful never to lose control each time your kid inquires you regarding grownups' pleasures. Keep cool and collected, irrespective of whether you find yourself surprised or uncomfortable. Losing your temper will possibly prevent future interactions as well as forestall the youngster trying to get directions down the road.

ADDRESSING COMMON MISCONCEPTIONS AND MYTHS

Whenever speaking about grownup pleasures with your child, it's necessary to take care of widely held misunderstandings together with myths to offer the kids genuine as well as dependable information. Just by removing such confusion, all of us assure our own young people obtain realistic as well as wholesome knowledge with regards to intimate overall health together with connections. This topic goal for you is to target various misconceptions and myths pertaining to sex and give support to allow both mothers and fathers to have these kinds of discussions proficiently.

Popping the Cherry

Explain the widespread belief related to popping the cherry. Tell your kids that there isn't any bodily cherry that interrupts the erotic activity. They need to know that the cherry refers to the hymen, which is a slim membrane present within the vagina. The hymen extends or tears the first time a female has sex or can even tear during sports actions or perhaps tampon insertion.

The Withdrawal Method Prevents Pregnancy

Dispel the fantasy that the withdrawal method is a trustworthy form of birth control. They need to know about the presence of pre-cum that is present before ejaculation. Pre-cum often includes semen and can cause unwanted pregnancy. Encourage them to make use of successful as well as dependable contraceptive techniques to avoid unexpected pregnancy.

Menstruation as the Ultimate Baby Barrier

It is a false belief that sex during the period decreases the possibility of conception. State that it's possible to end up pregnant even after having sex during menstruation, although less likely. Convince them that sperm can reside in the reproductive system for many days after the event, subsequently increasing the probability of conception should ovulation occur immediately following sexual contact.

Contracting STIs from a Toilet Seat

Refute the thought regarding contractible diseases via the toilet seat. Point out that virtually all STIs require immediate contact with infected body fluids, like via lovemaking action or maybe sharing contaminated needles. Reassure your kids that regular exposure to places doesn't increase the threat of getting hold of sickness through toilet structures and so forth.

It's Not an Orgasm if It's Not Vaginal

Disprove the conviction about climaxes are merely feasible via vaginal penetration. Stress they are often attained via numerous types of sensual arousal, such as clitoral excitement, oral sexual intercourse, and joint masturbating. Motivate the comprehension enjoyment plus climaxes might be experienced throughout diversified strategies.

There Are No Treatments for STIs

Repair the incorrect notion that there are zero remedies obtainable for STIs. Make clear that quite a few diseases, specifically chlamydia as well as gonorrhea, might be treated utilizing antibiotics. Highlight the significance connected with searching for professional treatment options in case the condition is suspected or identified.

Masturbation Is Bad for You

Challenge the incorrect belief that touching yourself will probably cause injury or wrongdoing. Make sure you keep in mind that touching oneself again is a normal as well as a wholesome area of human sexuality.

Guarantee youngsters this really is a harmless technique meant for personal pleasurable understanding physique along with experiencing bliss. Promote a judgment-free strategy toward self-gratification.

Sex Affects Athletic Performance

Fix the particular untrue idea that sexual activities damage sports' overall performance. Advise that we have seen absolutely no research to aid this specific declaration. Assure the young people that this will not have a negative impact on their ability to execute activities, toughness, or sports functionality.

DISCUSSING THE POTENTIAL RISKS OF EARLY SEXUAL ACTIVITY

Parents should always talk about prospective risks connected with early sexual activity along with teenagers. Simply by providing correct tips and creating positive surroundings, we could assist our teenagers in having knowledgeable options about their particular sexual health and well-being. This topic focuses on likely dangers related to early sexual activity and guides parents in discussing these risks with their kids in a supportive and reassuring manner.

Emotional Consequences

Early sexual relations are often followed by emotional consequences like remorse, a sense of guilt, or maybe uncertainty. Highlight the importance of being emotionally prepared for intimate relationships as well as valuing the significance of knowing and understanding one's own boundaries as well as emotions.

Physical Health Risks

Speak about prospective health pitfalls linked to early sexual activity, like STIs as well as unexpected pregnancies. Provide exact details regarding means of conception as well as great things about making use of barrier techniques, similar to condoms, toward lowering your chance connected with STIs as well as undesired pregnancies, as we discussed earlier.

Relationship Challenges

Discuss the fact that early sexual activities can bring up relationship complications, such as trouble with setting and keeping healthy boundaries, communication issues, as well as unbalanced power dynamics. Inspire open and respectful interaction, indicating the importance of consent, mutual respect, and shared decision-making in relationships.

Impact on Education and Future Goals

Talk to your teenagers about how early sexual behavior might affect education in addition to expected ambitions. Describe that getting involved in sexualized hobbies while young will take away through academic pursuits and disturb long-term aspirations. Support teens to target their personal growth and training, and also construct a solid base to get their future.

Legal Consequences

Tackle legal consequences connected with early sexual habits, especially those that involve underage activities or perhaps when it violates age of consent laws. Point out the need for recognizing and adhering to the legal minimum age so you can stay away from the potential legal ramifications associated with participating in sexual actions before the age of consent.

Emotional Intimacy and Relationship Development

Chat about the relevance involving emotional closeness plus relationship development preceding joining in sexual activities. Alert that sexual intimacy truly is a personal and significant aspect of a relationship and should be approached with care, trust, and understanding. Encourage your teenagers to prioritize emotional connection in addition to mutual respect in most of their relationships.

Impact on Mental Health

Talk about how early sexual activity can affect the frame of mental health. Let them know there exists an elevated threat connected with encountering worry, depression, and even reduced self-worth participating in sexual activity before one may be psychologically and intellectually prepared. Encourage your teenagers to prioritize their mental well-being and seek support if needed.

HANDLING QUESTIONS ABOUT SEXUAL ORIENTATION AND GENDER IDENTITY

Talking about sexual orientation along with gender identity together with your kids can be crucial in addition to validating conversation that will encourage comprehension, agreement, and assistance. By taking on these types of queries having openness, recognition, as well as exact details, we are able to set up a secure, safe, inclusive environment for kids to explore their own identities and foster empathy toward others. This topic's purpose is to guide parents through working with typical concerns pertaining to sexual orientation along with gender identity with kids.

What is Sexual Orientation?

Define the theory regarding human sexual orientation, focusing on the individual's emotionally charged, passionate, or even sexual attraction to other people. Examine various sexual preferences, such as heterosexual, homosexual, and bi-sexual, along with pansexual, although stress that every single individual's practical tastes and expertise differs.

What is Gender Identity?

Describe gender identification as an individual's profoundly considered idea regarding becoming a male or female, feminine, or something beyond the traditional dual principle regarding chromosomes. Make clear the fact that gender identity may not necessarily align with the actual assignment of sex given birth. Present the idea that each and every specific gender identity must be valued along with supporting individual choice.

Is It Normal to Question One's Sexual Orientation or Gender Identity?

Reassure your children that questioning one's sexual orientation or gender identity can be a normal component of self-discovery. Also, let them know that every single individual's journey regarding self-discovery differs.

Can Sexual Orientation or Gender Identity Change?

Explain that sexual orientation and gender identity are integral aspects on the inside. They are just a part of who you are—it doesn't go away or change no matter how old you get. And just like we celebrate all the cool things that make us special and unique individuals inside and out... embracing and accepting every bit of ourselves is so important, too!

How Can I Be Supportive of LGBTQ+ Individuals?

Have conversations about the necessity of establishing a helpful and inclusive atmosphere for LGBTQ+ people. Stress the importance of comprehension, sympathy, and understanding. Encourage your kid to oppose stereotypes, avert prejudice, and function as a dependable supporter of LGBTQ+ individuals.

Can Someone Be Both Gay and Transgender?

Communicate to your kids that sexual orientation and gender identity are discrete pieces of their individuality. Make clear to your children that it is possible for someone to be both homosexual and trans-gender since the libido definition deals with whom you fancy, whereas consciousness of personal self has to do with how you visualize yourself on the inside.

How Can I Show Support to Someone Questioning Their Identity?

Empower your kids by advising them to render aid to individuals questioning their sexual orientation or gender identity. Educate your children to lend an ear, provide reassurance, and respect their confidentiality since it's a sensitive matter for a few people. Advise kids to grow familiar with these issues and seek knowledge to better understand and support their friends or peers.

Can People Change Their Gender?

Instruct your children that transformation pertaining to one's gender requires private deliberation and several factors might call for consideration before a decision can be made about moving forward. Highlight the fact that not everyone chooses to transition altogether but nevertheless has a distinct outlook on things due to their inner awareness. Those who wish to proceed could experience numerous adjustments to their manner of living. Be mindful to stress the importance of respecting an individual's self-identified gender.

PROVIDING RESOURCES FOR FURTHER SUPPORT AND INFORMATION

Be sure that your children receive credible and dependable content if the necessity arises. Providing appropriate data will help them reach well-informed judgments relating to their life journeys. It helps to arm kids with useful materials so that they can deal with matters when the occasion occurs. This topic concentrates on providing info that promotes an optimistic and complete grasp of sexual health, connections, and concurrence. By giving reliable resources, parents could share with kids and encourage an all-round understanding of sexual health, relationships, and consent.

Planned Parenthood (www.plannedparenthood.org)

Planned Parenthood supplies sex health and fitness guidance pertaining to all age ranges. Their website provides varying facts consisting of academic information and other helpful sources across multiple subject areas, for instance, prophylactic solutions, affliction, approbation, and wholesome connections. The online functions contain both static and dynamic content, providing visitors with several study solutions on those themes above.

Advocates for Youth (www.advocatesforyouth.org)

Advocates for Youth is a nonprofit organization emphasizing the growth of adolescent sexual health and well-being. Their online presence features resources touching on sex health education, LGBTQ+ issues, reproductive rights, and advocacy. Additionally, the organization gives a detailed handbook designed specifically for parents and caregivers on how to talk to teenagers about sex.

Scarleteen (www.scarleteen.com)

Scarleteen provides inclusive sex education information and encouragement for kids aged 20 and below. Its website covers lots of varying matters, including sexual health, consent, relationships, and LGBTQ+ issues. Information comes across in formats geared toward more youthful patrons and without biased opinions thrown in.

Sex, Etc. (www.sexetc.org)

Sex, Etc., is a gang of youth members providing instructions on sex-related subjects and resources for teenagers searching for information written by others from their own generation. On their website, one can find articles, personal stories, and question-and-answer sections addressing various topics, such as puberty, relationships, contraception, and STIs. Young adults looking for tips coming from other youngsters would probably discover this website most helpful.

Amaze (www.amaze.org)

Amaze works to give extensive sexual guidance to young persons, employing moving imagery and additional learning components obtainable over the internet. You can view captivating video clips and resources. The website contains engaging videos covering a range of topics, including puberty, consent, body image, and healthy relationships. The content is age-appropriate and suitable for different developmental stages.

The Trevor Project (www.thetrevorproject.org)

The Trevor Project concentrates primarily on helping out LGBTQ+ teens through its website. It offers information on sexual orientation, gender identity, mental health, and crisis intervention services. It makes it easier for self-identifying LGBTQ+ individuals who are facing difficulties finding helpful hints appropriate for their individual cases.

Your Local Public Library

Prompt your children to drop by the neighborhood library, where they can find a variety of books on sexual health, relationships, consent, and LGBTQ+ issues. In addition, reference librarians will pick suggested manuals based on the age and interests of each child.

Teen Health Source (www.teenhealthsource.com)

Teen Health Source functions as a Canada-based platform delivering useful materials regarding adolescent sexual welfare destined for youth. Their website offers articles, fact sheets, and resources covering topics such as puberty, contraception, STIs, and healthy relationships. The data presented caters specifically to young ones' requirements and maintains openness toward the topic itself.

School-Based Sex Education Programs

Advise your kids to proactively take part in educational schemes carried out in academic institutions targeted at informing learners about sexual matters. Counselors or trainers available at schools usually provide consultations plus suggest extra learning materials.

By discussing most of these resources, kids are inspired to engage in continuous communication concerning erotic wellness and their total personalities. We encourage equitableness as well as back up our kids to make better choices while they travel their particular lovemaking growth and develop a secure and suitable appreciation associated with themselves as well as some others. We must ensure each of our kids acquires entry to exact data files, sustain, and instructions since they go after their very own intimate creation and assemble a good as well as thoughtful recognizing involving personally together with others.

CONCLUSION

Congratulations on finishing the book. You just explored a helpful and useful aid pertaining to parent or guardian conversations around the sensitive topic of sex guidance. This book constantly focused attention on the importance of unrestricted interaction with kids, truthful data, kindness, and sensitivity in producing wholesome mindsets and behaviors within the realms of sex, relationships, consent, and personal well-being.

We discussed the importance of establishing sincerity and creating an appropriate environment for the discussion of connections and sex remains essential. We explored various chapters: familiarizing with social media, online safety, concurrence, limits and preventative measures, sexual health and reproduction, facing challenges, and embracing diversity. Useful tips and comforting suggestions are presented in every chapter for raising kids to be prepared when communicating crucial subjects with them.

The key takeaway from this book is that having open and sincere conversations with your kids is vital for creating healthy mindsets regarding sex and bonds. If we construct an environement based on sincerity, admiration, and compassionate feelings, then we are able to direct our children toward coming to a decision and generating limits, plus maintaining strong bonds with them.

As we conclude this book, it is important to take some time to think about the main ideas and tools given in each chapter. Recall that you now possess adequate expertise and knowledge that will help you engage in rewarding and helpful conversations with your kids. Embrace the role of a trusted guide, supporting them as they explore their identities, make choices, and navigate the complexities of sex and relationships. You are now equipped with every tool needed, so take advantage and utilize them. Pay attention to their problems as well as queries, and present truthful and age-appropriate information. Grant your children the opportunity to arrive at choices on their own and assist them in creating balanced interactions.

If you benefited from reading this book and it has made a positive impact on your journey as a parent or caregiver, then please take a moment to share your thoughts by leaving a review on the Amazon platform. Your feedback will help others discover this resource and benefit from the knowledge and support it offers.

Thank you for embarking on this journey with this book. Don't forget that being a parent or guardian plays a substantial part in crafting future societal values via your efforts and actions today. We build an environment where adolescents are able to mature in a wholesome frame of mind by developing honest exchanges while practicing sympathy and regard toward one another. That results in grown-ups having improved views concerning affection and wellness in general.

Wishing you and your family a journey filled with love, understanding, and positive growth.

CHAPTER "GOOD WILL"

Helping others without expectation of anything in return has been proven to lead to increased happiness and satisfaction in life.

I would love to give you the chance to experience that same feeling during your reading or listening experience today...

All it takes is a few moments of your time to answer one simple question:

<u>Would you make a difference in the life of someone you've never met—without spending any money or seeking recognition for your good will?</u>

If so, I have a small request for you.

If you've found value in your reading or listening experience today, I humbly ask that you take a brief moment right now to leave an honest review of this book. It won't cost you anything but 30 seconds of your time— just a few seconds to share your thoughts with others.

Your voice can go a long way in helping someone else find the same inspiration and knowledge that you have.

Are you familiar with leaving a review for an Audible, Kindle, or e-reader book? If so, it's simple:

If you're on **Audible**: just hit the three dots in the top right of your device, click rate & review, then leave a few sentences about the book along with your star rating.

If you're reading on **Kindle** or an e-reader, simply scroll to the last page of the book and swipe up—the review should prompt from there.

If you're on a **Paperback** or any other physical format of this book, you can find the book page on Amazon (or wherever you bought this) and leave your review right there.

https://amazon.com/review/create-review/?&asin= B0CV4GMHJD

REFERENCES

Ashiana. (2020, January 17). *Emotional wellbeing of children: Why it matters to raise an emotionally balanced child*. Ashiana. https://www.ashianahousing.com/real-estate-blog/emotional-wellbeing-of-children-why-it-matters-to-raise-an-emotionally-balanced-child/

Boskey, E. (2020, February 16). *Top 10 reasons to support sex education in schools*. Verywell Health. https://www.verywellhealth.com/support-comprehensive-educa tion-schools-3133083

Butler, S. (2011). *Teaching communication in sex educa-tion: Facilitating teaching communication in sex education: Facilitating communication skills knowledge and ease of use communication skills knowledge and ease of use*. DePaul

University. https://via.library.depaul.edu/cgi/viewcon tent.cgi?article=1093&context=etd

Chernyak, P. (2017, February 9). *3 ways to handle your child's first crush.* WikiHow. https://www.wikihow.com/ Handle-Your-Child%27s-First-Crush

Cherry, K. (2021, December 1). *6 different types of relationships you may find yourself in.* Verywell Mind. https://www.verywellmind.com/6-types-of-relation ships-and-their-effect-on-your-life-5209431

Desiraju, M. (2018). *Your child's growth (for parents).* Kidshealth. https://kidshealth.org/en/parents/childs-growth.html

Dowshen, S. (2015). *Understanding puberty (for parents).* Kidshealth. https://kidshealth.org/en/parents/under standing-puberty.html

Fishman, S. (2022, July 22). *3 power dynamics in relationships and how to overcome them.* Psych Central. https:// psychcentral.com/relationships/power-dynamics-in-relationships

Ford, M. (2022, December 7). *Create a judgment-free zone.* Center for Parent and Teen Communication. https://parentandteen.com/parenting-judgment-free-zone/

Foster, T. (2020, February 3). *15 negotiation tips to help you save your relationships.* Success Consciousness. https://www.successconsciousness.com/blog/relation ships/negotiation-tips-to-save-relationships/

Furnival, C. (n.d.). *Teaching kids about healthy friendships & boundaries.* Pesi. Retrieved July 18, 2023, from https://www.pesi.com/blog/details/1962/teaching-kids-about-healthy-friendships-boundaries

G, A. (2015, August 7). *8 steps to better family communication.* Froddo. http://www.froddo.com/8-steps-to-better-family-communication

Gordon, S. (2019, August 21). *Many young girls are unprepared for puberty - here's how to help.* Verywell Family. https://www.verywellfamily.com/how-to-prepare-girls-for-puberty-4689051

Gordon, S. (2021, August 31). *Why teaching media literacy is important.* Verywell Family. https://www.very wellfamily.com/media-literacy-how-to-teach-kids-to-be-critical-consumers-5181306

Greenan, K. A. (2019). Comfort levels and communication styles of sexual health educators: An interdisciplinary study. *Academic Journal of Interdisciplinary Studies, 8*(2), 1–13. https://doi.org/10.2478/ajis-2019-0011

Gruber, E., & Grube, J. W. (2000). Adolescent sexuality and the media: A review of current knowledge and implications. *The Western Journal of Medicine, 172*(3), 210–214. https://www.ncbi.nlm.nih.gov/pmc/articles/PMC1070813/

HACEY. (2022, March 14). *Sex education for children: Parents' responsibilities digitalizing sexual reproductive health services access for young people.* HACEY. https://hacey.org/blog/sex-education-for-children-parents-responsibilities/

Hakanson, C. (2019, August 25). *13 good reasons to talk to kids about sex: The advantages of sex education.* Sex Ed Rescue. https://sexedrescue.com/advantages-of-sex-education/

Herrity, J. (2019). *Negotiation skills: Definition and examples.* Indeed. https://www.indeed.com/career-advice/career-development/negotiation-skills

Khan, S. (2022, January 28). *How to teach media literacy to kids.* Edtech Review. https://www.edtechreview.in/trends-insights/insights/how-to-teach-media-literacy-to-kids/

Laurence, E. (2022, June 13). *When should you have "the talk" with your kids?* Forbes Health. https://www.forbes.com/health/family/when-should-you-have-the-talk/

Liquin, E. G., & Lombrozo, T. (2020). Explanation-seeking curiosity in childhood. Current *Opinion in Behavioral Sciences, 35,* 14–20. https://doi.org/10.1016/j.cobeha.2020.05.012

Lyness, D. (2018). *Dealing with peer pressure (for kids).* Kids Health. https://kidshealth.org/en/kids/peer-pressure.html

Mind Tools Content Team. (2022). *Mutual respect.* Mind Tools. https://www.mindtools.com/adilccw/mutual-respect

Miron-Shatz, T., & Yaniv, H. (2022). Digital consent: Engaging patients with plain language and better communication. *BMJ,* o2378. https://doi.org/10.1136/bmj.o2378

Morin, A. (2013, November 16). *15 things to talk about in A healthy relationship.* Lifehack. https://www.lifehack.org/articles/communication/15-things-talk-about-healthy-relationship.html

National Society for the Prevention of Cruelty to Children. (2020). *Talking to your child about online safety.* NSPCC. https://www.nspcc.org.uk/keeping-children-safe/online-safety/talking-child-online-safety/

Pearl, E., & Joseph, B. (2018, April). *Teaching kids to be smart about social media (for parents).* Kids Health.

https://kidshealth.org/en/parents/social-media-smart
s.html

Pfeuffer, C. (2020, October 15). *How to answer just about every sex question your child could ever ask*. SheKnows. https://www.sheknows.com/health-and-wellness/arti cles/1140392/how-to-answer-sex-questions-from-kids/amp/

Ping, H. L. (2019, February 14). *The rightful role of parents in sex education*. Today. https://www.todayon line.com/voices/rightful-role-parents-sex-education

Potnis, N. (2019, September 25). *Why the sex talk is so awkward for parents and children*. Bingedaily. https:// www.bingedaily.in/article/why-the-sex-talk-is-so-awkward-for-parents-and-children

Prochaska, A. (2021, March 20). *Porn and unrealistic expectations*. Linkedin. https://www.linkedin.com/ pulse/porn-unrealistic-expectations-alyssa-prochaska/

Raising Children Network. (2017, December 11). *Physical changes in puberty: Girls and boys*. Raising Children Network. https://raisingchildren.net.au/pre-teens/ development/puberty-sexual-development/physical-changes-in-puberty

Ritchie, M. B. (2019, January 25). *Kids and crushes: How*

to handle them. TulsaKids Magazine. https://www.tulsakids.com/grade-school-crushes/

Scheel, J. (2019, January 2). *Talking about sex with your children: Who is uncomfortable?* Pychology Today. https://www.psychologytoday.com/us/blog/sex-is-language/201901/talking-about-sex-your-children-who-is-uncomfortable?amp

Schiedel, B. (2018, January 24). *This is how you talk to kids about their private parts.* Today's Parent. https://www.todaysparent.com/kids/school-age/this-is-how-you-talk-to-kids-about-their-private-parts/

Schmidt, C. (2018, March 19). *How and why to talk to your kids about their private parts.* Orlando Health. https://www.arnoldpalmerhospital.com/content-hub/how-and-why-to-talk-to-your-kids-about-their-private-parts

Smith, S. (2017, September 28). *25 types of relationships that you might encounter.* Marriage Advice. https://www.marriage.com/advice/relationship/types-of-relationships/

Spicer, S. (2018, May 1). *How to handle your kid's body odour.* Today's Parent. https://www.todaysparent.com/kids/body-odour-and-kids/

Tatter, G. (2018, December 19). *Consent at every age | harvard graduate school of education*. Harvard. https://www.gse.harvard.edu/ideas/usable-knowledge/18/12/consent-every-age

Tiwary, A. (2021, March 28). *The importance of normalizing conversation around sex - hints of life*. Hints of Life. https://hintsoflife.com/importance-of-normalizing-conversation-around-sex/

Van Ouytsel, J., Lu, Y., Ponnet, K., Walrave, M., & Temple, J. R. (2019). Longitudinal associations between sexting, cyberbullying, and bullying among adolescents: Cross-lagged panel analysis. *Journal of Adolescence, 73*, 36–41. https://doi.org/10.1016/j.adolescence.2019.03.008

Made in the USA
Las Vegas, NV
03 December 2024